Birdsplaining

Jasmine Donahaye is author of six books, including the award-winning memoir *Losing Israel*. Her work has appeared in the *New York Times* Modern Love column, in the *Guardian* and on BBC Radio 4. She is Emeritus Professor of Creative Writing at Swansea University, and a Fellow of the Learned Society of Wales.

ALSO BY JASMINE DONAHAYE

Misappropriations
Self-Portrait as Ruth
Whose People? Wales, Israel, Palestine
The Greatest Need: The Creative Life and Troubled Times of Lily Tobias, a Welsh Jew in Palestine
Losing Israel

Birdsplaining

A Natural History

JASMINE DONAHAYE

Parthian, Cardigan SA43 1ED
www.parthianbooks.com
First published in 2023 by New Welsh Rarebyte
This edition published by Parthian in 2025
© Jasmine Donahaye
Print ISBN 978-1-91-714032-4
Ebook ISBN 978-1-91-714011-9
Editor: Gwen Davies
Typeset by Syncopated Pandemonium
Printed by 4edge
Published with the financial support of the Books Council of
Wales
British Library Cataloguing in Publication Data
A cataloguing record for this book is available from the British
Library.
Printed on FSC accredited paper

To Dr Edwards, Dr McKeogh, and Dr Mohammed

Contents

Birdsplaining: A Note Before Reading

Birds explain nothing to me. I am often unsure what they are or why they matter. The presiding mode in this book is therefore inevitably one of uncertainty. Perhaps the response to that uncertainty might be, *Go do some research! Make up your mind. Enough with the words 'perhaps', 'maybe', 'I wonder whether....'* That would be fair. Many people present their ideas and opinions with the certainty of expertise, and many do it well. I am grateful for expertise – that form of knowledge accrued over years of research, experience, engagement with others' work, and learning from mistakes – and I am glad to be able to rely on it (my doctor's, for example). But many pass off opinion as expertise. Certainty is certainly not authority.

Uncertainty is also a way I have of relating to others in a more personal way. I often find myself asking, 'Does that make sense?' after I've made a statement or answered a question, whether in a private or public setting. I used to kick myself for doing that, because I thought it was an embarrassing equivalent to uptalk, for which young women in particular are criticised. But perhaps uptalk has a similar function: it seems to ask the other person, *Are you coming with me along this conversational path? Are you still here?* I realise that I ask if something makes sense not because I am unsure of what I'm saying, but because I'm unsure if I have expressed it clearly, or if the other person has understood. It's a form of checking in, an invitation to an exchange or a response, an *are you with me? What do you make of that?*

Some might object to the term 'mansplaining', from which birdsplaining derives, as anything but inviting, instead seeing it as reductive, judgemental, and even coercive – a new form of silencing. I have some sympathy with that objection. After all, I have mounted a personal war and now a rearguard action against the term 'relatable' (possibly this war is, in itself, relatable). 'Relatable', to many who use the word, is a neutral term that allows you to identify a feeling of connection to someone (a person, a character) or something (a film, an attitude, a book – perhaps even this book). But to me it suggests that the only valuable characters, experiences or cultural productions are those that you can in some way identify with. It seems to enable a maybe dangerous value system that gives precedence to what is comfortable and familiar, over what might be alienating or difficult. A wholescale loss of critical thinking, complexity and nuance appears to me to be at stake, although defenders of the term might counter that it carries a whole range of complexity and nuance.

The way in which I find use of the term 'relatable' to be simplistic, reductive, and judgemental probably maps quite tidily onto the way in which some see the use of the term 'man-splaining'. Mansplaining is certainly a judgemental term. It laughs at men – or, when a man uses it about himself, he is often apologising, or rueful, and laughs at himself. It carries layers of social observation, and subtle humour, even as it undoubtedly simplifies and reduces. But its usefulness depends on a shared way of seeing. Those whom it aggravates perhaps reveal themselves to hold a view of the world in which men are permitted to explain things to women unasked, without any awareness that they might be exercising a power that they deny they have.

Of course, new words – mansplaining, relatable, perhaps even birdsplaining, if it were to catch on – can be threatening. A new word can change values; it can change our understanding of the past. After Rebecca Solnit's 'Men Explain Things to Me' appeared in 2008, the new term it gave rise to did just that. For some, an allegedly innocent (and now notorious) 1950s Texas campus sculpture of a man and a woman has become 'mansplaining' personified: the sculpture depicts a man standing with one foot up on a bench, actively explaining to a listening woman who is passively seated with a book (no doubt he is explaining the book itself). Retroactively, the meanings of the sculpture, and perhaps the intentions of the sculptor, have changed as a result of what it has come to represent.

Part of the effectiveness of the term mansplaining is its adaptability to other situations where there is an imbalance of power – where there is the member of a majority group presuming to 'explain' to a member of a disempowered minority what they ought to think or feel or do, or what their predicament really means ('whitesplaining', 'goysplaining'). The derivatives proliferate as a kind of shorthand to how social power is exercised in so many situations.

Certainly, in some of these essays I react to privilege and power exercising its prerogatives to talk over, talk down to, and explain others' experience for them, and to disregard others' expertise.

'Birdsplaining' as a term can represent how that plays out in the world of birdwatching. But I have tried to put the term birdsplaining to a more constructive use as well, exploring birds as a means of understanding social relationships and human relationships to the living world of which we are a part, and seeking to do something different from presuming to assert authority or claim expertise.

I have no claim on expertise except that of my own experience, and, as with everyone else, no one has authority about my own experience except me. So exploring some ideas based on personal experience seemed a sensible place to start. A lot of how I make sense of experience has to do with the animate world in general, and birds in particular – hence the term birdsplaining also, for me, denotes understanding experience through birds.

There's a lot of heated taking up of positions based on instant expertise, bolstered by a bit of overnight googling, but I prefer a conversation to an argument, which is so often merely a series of reactions to opinions with opinions (no doubt I'm guilty of some of that here too). By contrast, a conversation can be a shared exploration. These essays are an attempt at starting that kind of conversation – more a case of 'May I tell you what I've been thinking?' than 'Here's what you need to know I know.' Of course there's no getting around the fact that writing for publication is an offering of opinion without invitation – except that a book by its nature is only ever an invitation to read, not an injunction.

1. Reading the Signs

In the waiting room, a man is holding the edges of his newspaper so tightly that he has crumpled the pages. He stares at the news, his eyes not moving. Somewhere beyond the pale beech veneer door with its heavy steel handle, the woman he loves is stripping off her shirt, undoing her bra, laying them on a chair; she is stepping up to the machine, leaning into it as instructed, trying to relax her arm, which the radiographer places out of the way like a discarded scarf. She is pulling her other breast away from the descending plate; she winces as the plates meet, and this organ of pleasure and nourishment, slack and misshapen, is squeezed flat. She gasps at the surprising grip, and the man she loves is weeping in the waiting room, staring at the page of his paper which he has not yet turned, which he will never turn. What is happening in the world has blurred and cannot be retrieved. All this week and next there will be no news but the static of a radio caught between stations.

In a few minutes, she'll be done. Turning away from the radiographer, she'll hook-and-eye her bra in a strange new modesty, and pull on her shirt. She'll come back through that heavy door and he will stand up, fast, laying down the paper without folding it. They'll go home. He'll make them tea, and they'll drink it together; they will lie down together and make love quietly, mid-morning, not knowing what is to come, whether this autumn, this shit-and-maggots season, is the shit-and-maggots season of their love.

What did they secretly count or note, what private readings and understandings did they create out of what they saw as they drove here this morning? *If the sun breaks through the cloud... if the traffic light turns green before I count to twenty-five... if there's somewhere to park straight away, then everything's going to be OK; she's going to be all right.* And what dread clutched him when, by the count of twenty-five, the light had not after all changed, nor by thirty, by thirty-five? How did he qualify it, extending the permissible count? And how could he ignore the sign when, afterwards, a single magpie flew up from the red dogwood by the used-car forecourt?

Soon it will be my turn: they'll call my name, and

I'll go through the door, as I do every autumn. All summer it has been building to this: the turn of the year, and what I want to forget.

The dull clustered blackberries have begun to bulge at the edge of decomposition, and sycamore leaves shrivel at the edges, not so much changing colour as losing colour. Tortoiseshell butterflies have started to explore the cool interior of the house, but I don't want them with me, or their signal of the year's end. They creep into small gaps, into the cracks in cobwebby beams, dark niches and retreats where they will hole up but from which they emerge sometimes on a harshly bright day in winter, when the ground is glittering with a crunch of frost. I know they can't survive, but they batter at the condensation-wet window panes, wanting out into that killing light.

After two years, after three, after seven, the signs of these days around the equinox remain the same – and the regret: that I didn't go, immediately; didn't drop everything, grab my passport, drive the five hours to the airport, catch a plane, any combination of planes, fly the twenty-four hours from Heathrow or Manchester to Dubai or Hong Kong or Singapore, and from there the eight to Brisbane – so that I might have seen her; so that I might have held her; so that I might have told her.

On the way here to the city for the test, this Tuesday morning, for my annual ritual reading of the signs, I drove in slashing rain, then sun through rain, then sun breaking through to shine on the heavy cloud massed above the city – burnished dread light, a kind of apocalyptic mid-storm reprieve. The herring gulls had come inland, flashing white against the dark sky, delighting to let themselves be shunted, and then turning about into the wind as if in defiance of that element we hardly know at all – wind like the force of death or birth; wind entering you, surrounding you, embracing and throwing you, like a man who loves with rage, unable to contain the incredulity of his hurt, of his confusion, yanking you to him, and flinging you from him. Then the gulls, letting go their defiance, slipped sideways into the wind's violent embrace.

No matter what I see in them, I know that birds are sovereign, autonomous, not subject to the projections of my small needs and anxieties. The natural world is not glorious, a respite, but a matter of implacable drives. Still I read it for signs as I have always done – as I did some thirty years ago when a cloud of tortoiseshell butterflies emerged from the patch of nettles on a late September day, the morning I was to leave with a man I hardly knew. What were they a sign of – the cliché of freedom that I was about to lose, or a mad, hopeless dash towards frost? Ten years later, sitting on the top step of the stairs to the basement, wondering how I was going to explain my injury if I went to A&E, realising that it would have to heal itself, as I would have to heal the rift again, I remembered that day watching from the upstairs window as the tortoiseshells emerged from the patch of nettle.

Yesterday there was a bird in the house. It was just a small sound at first, a shifting in the chimney. Then, later, I heard it in the pipe behind the woodburning stove. Somehow a bird had got in through the opening under the chimney cap, had become confused, or been injured, or had dropped down inside the pipe for shelter, or as an escape from a predator. Then it became trapped in the dark, unable to spread its wings to fly back up, unable perhaps to see light beyond the bend in the pipe. It shuffled there behind the stove, scratching with small claws.

I thought I might have to sit there all day listening to its efforts to get out, hearing the stirring of soot, its claws scraping on the metal pipe, imagining its feathers blackening, bedraggled – by degrees losing energy, losing time, losing hope. And then afterwards I would have begun to smell its death.

But somehow, perhaps seeing the light through the narrow flue, it struggled out of the pipe and into the stove. It stirred up the ash, and ticked with a small beak at the tarred glass of the door. I knelt before it, supplicant, and the tiny ashy creature squatted, exhausted, wings spread, beak open, watching me. I got up and closed all the curtains and opened the back door, and then I unlatched the stove door, and the bird flung itself towards the light outside.

I know what a bird in the house means. This morning, driving down, warding off bad news, I discounted the solitary magpie clattering into an ash tree, and her ominous message. Determined, willing the outcome to be joy, I looked for a pair with their oracular capacity, hoping that they might erase the sign the first magpie gave me, but one after another they told me *sorrow*, *sorrow*, *sorrow* – that one, rising from the fox carcass; that one by the slaughterhouse, launching itself across the road; that one perched on a telegraph pole, watching me pass.

Everything else was a sign to something I could not read: the curlews stalking in the stubble; a pale fox trotting along an invisible path; a heron awkward and humped on a rusting gate, and the purple willowherb merely bare and drying canes.

Now, waiting for my name to be called, thinking

of that ashy, unrecognisable creature ticking at the inside of the stove glass, I tell myself that there have been other birds in the house and no death occurred – and deaths occur at any time, all the time, so why suppose it's to do with me? Nevertheless, in unguarded moments, bearing in on me is the certain knowledge that a bird in the house foretells not any death but a specific death: a death in the family. Scrabbling away from it, I lie to myself that people have always had birds in the house: wild linnets or canaries in cages; chickens scratching underfoot; an African grey parrot or a turquoise and gold macaw climbing on its stand, brought back from overseas by ship, outliving its owner. And the swallows that come in, every spring, sweeping around the open door, looking for somewhere to nest: surely they erase the meaning of a bird in the house that inexplicably appears inside when all the openings are shut, flailing at the window, desperate to escape – as the soul from the body at the end.

I learned at the age of ten how to hold a bird. At the ringing station on Beachy Head, caught in the mist-nets strung across the tops of the chalk cliffs, the birds hung entangled, or writhed and struggled, convulsed with the effort to get free, and then went still. Conserving energy, only their dark glossy eyes were alert, watching my approach. I learned how to tell the sex, ruffling a finger over the soft feathers of the vent, though I don't recall the details. I was too young but not young enough to be interested in their organs of defecation or reproduction.

I don't recall what a bird's sex looks like, though I kept cage birds – a chattering budgie; zebra finches, coloured like clowns, red-beaked and striped, endlessly hopping and beeping like some advertisement for long-life batteries. At the commercial aviary twenty miles from home, I drifted like a lover heartsick with desire through the corridors of cages that contained doves and canaries, cockatiels and rainbow lorikeets, and screeching sulphur-crested cockatoos which climbed up the bars using beak and feet, revealing grey knobbed tongues and scaly toes.

We loved birds, my sister and I. We saved up for our budgies and finches and brought them home in small sturdy cardboard boxes which closed crisply with a flap at one end. I sat in the back seat, buckled in and keeping as still as I could against the movement of the car, feeling the weight of the new bird shift in the box from one end to the other, hearing the tiny scratch of its claws. I loved the paraphernalia of cage birds, too – the heavy bags of seed, brittle white eye-shapes of cuttlefish bone, the nubbed sprays of dry millet, the water bottles that slotted with a blue plastic tongue through the wires of the cage front and snapped into place in the tight metal hoop of the clasp.

The budgies and zebra finches didn't last long. Nor did my terrapins, which slowed in the cold green-fogged water of their uncleaned tank, and then went still. My sister had a cut-throat, a bloody-necked finch; he also died. In the aviary outside the back door the quails died, taken by rats. After the aviary was floored in wire netting, the rats tunnelled underneath and ogled the new tiny flightless quails leaping in alarm as though through fear alone they might regain the lost art of becoming airborne.

For a little while, I was devout, changing the water every day, cleaning the cages out, but soon I drifted away into neglect, and my birds hopped back and forth from perch to perch, from perch to wire cage front, from wire to floor to perch, never flying more than two seconds. The zebra finches compensated by nesting frantically, nesting endlessly. They built and laid and built again on top of eggs, in a pathological compulsion to reproduce, and a compulsion to end it at the same time, to smother the young before they'd even hatched – and, later, to smother their young before they were even laid. Egg-bound, the females sickened and died, one by one, and the males hopped and fluttered and beeped alone, and then they too sickened and died.

She died of course – three days after the phone call, at the autumn equinox, before I had a chance to see her, before I had the chance to talk to her. Even if I had gone straight to the airport I would not have got there in time. But I already knew the outcome, because the day before the phone call I had got up in the morning and come downstairs in the closed house and found a wren battering against the inside of the bathroom window. I caught it, frantic and scrabbling, and I held it, and I took it outside, and I knew my sister was going to die.

Here in the city, the trees have begun to turn. I realise that once again it is merely days till the anniversary of my sister's death, and I think of the single magpies foretelling sorrow, and it catches me suddenly, sharp as though it happened a mere week ago, the intensity of the loss. Because the losses still accumulate, as each of our experiences together dies – like the memory of sitting beside her with the bird boxes, now fading because it is no longer shared.

In the waiting room, it is my turn: the pale door opens, and the nurse calls my name. I go through and hear the door close heavily behind me as I prepare for the indignity of having my breasts lifted and draped and pulled and then squashed flat as though they are accidental appendages that hardly belong to me.

My sister's death has increased my risk, so each year in the autumn near the anniversary of her death I face not the possibility but the certainty of my own mortality, as every woman in that waiting room does. Every woman preparing herself, baring herself, submitting to the machinery, is facing what my sister was too afraid to face: that the reading of the signs might tell her what she feared was true.

I never told her about my own particular fear, because I too did not recognise it as fear: it was an element I lived in, like the gulls in the wind. I navigated its swell, its ebb and flow, waiting for it to peak and subside. I have never since known an intimacy like that. *It will be OK*, I told myself, the last time, sitting at the top of the stairway down to the basement. On my shoulder, whispering in my ear, there was a small hawk, telling me *repair repair repair*. It was a sparrowhawk, hooded, belled, like something out of TH White. I was suspended from my life, knowing that if I just did the right thing, if I managed to interpret the signs he was giving me, it would be OK: I'd be safe, for a bit. And that time, the last time, for a short while the knowledge of choice was intoxicating.

I knew what I had to do; I knew if I did it, the reward would be great. I could choose to mend the breach. I always could choose that. I always had mended the breach. If I gave him a way out, apologised, said it was my fault, everything would be repaired, and I would be safe again.

There is nothing like the naked intimacy of violence, when all that you fear is realised, and all pretence has been blown aside. And when you have taken the blame, abased yourself, crept on your belly like a muddied, bedraggled fox at bay, and the master of hounds has whipped off his dogs – for he is always both hunter and saviour – there is nothing like the intimacy of reconciliation after violence. When fear lifts, when you have asked for redemption, and he has given you redemption, you could not be closer, you could never feel more full of trust – for he is stunned by his capacity to lose control, appalled that it has happened; he is solicitous and tender, and full of regret. No one can know what the two of you know. You can't share with anyone but one another this trust, the unbreakable privacy of this secret shared culpability, and the heady, light relief when you are, for those few moments – minutes, maybe half a day or a day, until it begins to fall away again – safe.

*

By the time I come out of the clinic the storm has blown inland, and the gulls have returned to the shore. Rooks and jackdaws are turning on their backs in the wind above the dirty farm where the three-legged dog always leaps barking at my front wheels. Full of dread, I am for one moment reprieved by a pair of magpies, and my heart leaps up with the terrified optimism of the quails in the aviary.

While I wait for the test results, that long fortnight as the year shifts towards winter, the autumn becomes rot and chaos. The kite turning above something that has drowned in the torrential rain means nothing more than its own hunger. The hawthorn, heavy with berries the colour of old blood, points to earlier weather conditions, not to the weather conditions I project – the hard winter that no longer ever comes. The real story that the dying world is telling is a story of eating and shitting, of rutting and giving birth, of threat and fear, of dying and rotting and beginning again, and, after the cycle ends, the compulsion to go on.

When at last the letter arrives, telling me of my reprieve, as it does each year for another year, my sister's death is behind me, my own mortality is at bay, and suddenly, freed from fear, I am alive, sharply alive – as I was after violence, after everything nameless and bulging was made real. How exquisitely he could love me then. And how exquisitely I too could love in that temporary, heady release from the clamp of fear.

I think of the man in the waiting room, weeping behind his newspaper, as the woman he loved was submitting to the investigation of her body, and I feel for him a kind of tender longing, wondering if I can ever have a love like theirs. Because I know, now, that those dark eyes, that small beak ticking at the window of the stove, that unrecognisable ashy bird, was not looking out of its own life, or out of its own cage, but into mine.

2. Field Guides

At the back of the second-hand bookshop in Aberystwyth, there's a small room that is densely packed with the published legacy of that great invention, natural history. The books range from early formative accounts that laid the groundwork of disciplines as diverse as botany, marine biology and ornithology, to the most recent development, the nature memoir. In old editions and new, in leather and board and paperback, they line the shelves and lie stacked on the floor, in boxes and on tables. Usually I'll drift about for as long as I can there in the back room, leafing longingly through volumes I can't afford, and I am never able to leave without buying something about birds. The room smells of books once damp, now dry: a memory of leaking attic roofs and softened cardboard boxes, of estate sales and glass cases displaying egg collections and stuffed sparrowhawks and otters, of foxed pages and frayed stitching, abraded paper pulped by silverfish, for whom a bookshop like this must be an Eden.

While I browse, there is the harsh *hark hark hark* of herring gulls on the chimneys and roofs, an insistent loud crooning of feral pigeons, and a continual rattle across the conservatory roof, which is greened with a suggestion of the buddleia that takes root high up the walls inside railway stations – only here the green is from the pigeons.

I spent hours poring over bird books as a child. It started so early, the consulting of field guides, that it's hard for me to imagine an orientation to the world without them. My mother, uncertain in her knowledge and her new language as an immigrant, looked everything up; my father consulted the bird book to confirm and tick what he already thought he knew. But to me, when I was young, the field guide offered a vision of what I might hope one day to see.

On the shelf of second-hand field guides, those nominal pocket guides that only the capacious pockets of old mackintoshes could accommodate, I spot the brown hessian spine of an old Collins guide, *A Field Guide to the Birds of Britain and Europe*. I pull it off the shelf and open it. There's the rush of early, almost preverbal recognition that is like a breath, like a shiver: I'm three again, sitting on my father's lap, my brother and sister on either side, all looking at this same field guide. I know what the endpapers will depict before I leaf back to the beginning: the inside front cover shows a white background, with black silhouettes of common British birds perched on fence posts and in leafless trees and on three overhead lines. The inside of the back cover shows the same silhouetted birds in flight.

I have a hard time restraining myself when I hand it over to Martin, the proprietor, and pay the £2, exclaiming, 'We had this book when I was very young – well, obviously not this particular copy....' Martin glances at me with something like recognition and pity as he hands me the change. Evidently, he's witnessed this excited nostalgia before.

But when I get home and search through old black-and-white photographs for the record of that moment I remembered, I discover that my memory was wrong. We did have this very book, either its first or second edition, but it's my sister who is sitting on my father's lap, looking at the illustrations with him, my brother to one side, leaning over, looking at what my father is pointing out. My father has a pen in his other hand; he is about to add a tick to something we've just seen – at Weirwood Reservoir perhaps, or walking in the beech forest at Wych Cross. But I am not involved: I am standing off to one side playing with toy jewellery – a huge ring, a handful of bangles, and a little plastic jewellery case. I am absorbed in the jewellery, and can't even see the book.

Perhaps I have conflated a memory of that photograph with another, of my sister and me in velvet dresses, one on each of my father's knees, sitting at the table which is set with table mats depicting blue tits and chaffinches. Our Happy Families cards were birds; our puzzles and family excursions were birds. Birds were so much the natural order of things when I was a child that I never noticed it, and the field guide was so much part of the natural order that I internalised its patterns and relationships without ever noticing them either.

But now, when I open the book again at random on a page of finches – the red bullfinch, pale linnet, redpoll, twite, grosbeak, and crossbill – those patterns and relationships stand out starkly, and are impossible to ignore. In each illustration except that of the twite, the female is perched behind the male. Where his posture is upright, bold, declarative, she is bent over, submissive and demure. The twite is represented only by a single bird, identified as male, although – like the bullfinch and redpoll – the male and female twite differ from one another. Overleaf, the hawfinch, brambling, greenfinch and siskin are depicted the same way, with the horizontal female behind the upright male, while the goldfinch and citril finch each show one bird, with the note 'sexes similar'. Elsewhere it's even more marked: the male always appears in the foreground, upright, and the female is horizontal or dipped downward or even crouched down, in the position she might assume for mating; half of her is always obscured by the male. As with the twite, often only the male and the juvenile are illustrated, even though they differ from the female. If you were lucky enough to see a female ortolan bunting in the field you could not identify her – she has been erased.

Perhaps it's not surprising. Birdwatching has always been predominantly a male interest, and bird books are predominantly written and illustrated by men. This guide, the third edition, published in 1974, is dedicated to the authors' 'long-suffering wives'; below the dedication is a quotation from *The Merry Wives of Windsor*: 'She laments, sir... her husband / goes this morning a-birding.' Those authors are heirs of the men who determined how we apprehend the breathing, growing world around us – small groups of Oxbridge graduates and Anglican ministers who formed clubs that admitted new members by invitation only, who wrote voluminously to one another, traded skins and eggs and specimens, furthering the aims of empire abroad, and experimenting with empiricism at home, where their wives and daughters wrote up their catalogues and dusted their display cabinets. Of the ninety-one people identified in *Biographies for Birdwatchers: The Lives of those Commemorated in Western Palearctic Bird Names*, only three are women.

I check my other Collins field guide – this one, first published in 1972, has a larger geographic range: *The Birds of Britain and Europe with North Africa and the Middle East*. Here, the female bullfinch is perched below instead of behind the male. Above them, the postures and placement of the male and female siskin aesthetically mimic theirs. Next to the bullfinches perch the greenfinches: the female below the male, the juvenile below the female. On the next page the male hawfinch is in the foreground, partly obscuring the female hawfinch, whose head is decorously bent. Below them the pattern of the desert finches is the same. Where the females of some species are in the foreground, their posture is horizontal, or they are below, not above the male. Even if the male and female of the species are the same size, she is often shown smaller, in the background; or, if the differences occur only on the head, or head and breast, this is all of her that is illustrated. More suggestive yet, with some species such as the wheatears – hooded, pied, mourning, red-rumped – the females are shown a third of the size of the males; only the males are also illustrated in flight. There are exceptions, but in the vast majority of illustrations of sexually dimorphic birds the male dominates, the female is secondary.

The text in the 1972 edition mirrors the relationships shown in the illustrations. Each begins with the male, and the female is identified in terms of deviation from him. She constitutes what she lacks of his. Her colouring is paler, or duller, or browner, or greener; she lacks (the word is used over and over) the white wing bar of the male, or the moustache, or the black cap. His colours are bold; hers are tinges or washes. The male bullfinch, for example, 'is unmistakeable with black cap and red underparts', and the 'pinker female and juvenile almost equally so'.

Of course it is useful to identify the female and male of the species in relation to one another, as the texts tend to do, for that is the closest physical relationship that exists. With a few exceptions (phalaropes, for example), in bird species that are sexually dimorphic the male is indeed more strongly coloured than the female. You cannot describe them comparatively without observing those brighter/

duller, bolder/paler, more distinct/less defined binaries of sexual difference. But the illustrations also position the males of close species in relation to one another for identification purposes, while the females of related species (the various female wheatears, for example), which are much harder to distinguish from one another, are obscured. Not only are they explicitly a lower priority for identification but they become difficult to identify at all.

For years, until I consulted a newer field guide, I had difficulty distinguishing between male and female sparrowhawks. In my 1972 guide, the size of the sparrowhawk is given as a range – 11 to 15 inches – but the text does not state that the female is much larger than the male, that the female differs in greater values, not lesser ones. It is not because this was unknown at the time. The five-volume *Handbook of British Birds*, published between 1939 and 1941, is explicit: it identifies the female sparrowhawk as 'conspicuously larger' than the male.

The omission in my 1972 guide might simply have been an oversight (after all, a great deal of space is given to describing other differences in this species), but, taken together with the descriptions and illustrations elsewhere, the omission is suggestive. Something in how the authors saw the world meant that they overlooked this significant detail which disrupted a pattern, perhaps in a way that had uncomfortably echoed disruptions in the patterns of their own lives in the 1960s and early 1970s (perhaps it is also no accident that this larger female is a predator).

Regardless of what caused that oversight, the effect it had on me is clear: how I saw and therefore identified sparrowhawks was for many years confused. A way of looking at the world had determined how I could see; it made it hard for me to observe a difference which, once identified, was impossible *not* to see.

Newer field guides don't replicate these patterns. The British Trust for Ornithology book, *British Birds*, published by Collins in 2015, shows male and female birds in separate illustrations, and these are photographs, not drawings. Still, the authors are all men, and of the forty-four named photographers, only two, or possibly three, are women. The authors of the RSPB *Handbook of British Birds*, published by Bloomsbury in 2014, are also all men, although one or two of the six illustrators are women. Here, too, male and female birds are shown in separate illustrations of equal size. Those human social patterns of the 1960s and 1970s no longer determine the relationships in the field guides – but they shaped me, and shaped how I perceived the world.

Now, aware of them, I observe myself observing birds, and I see the more insidious damage that these patterns have caused. One dark snowy morning in February, I watch two female bullfinches on a bending piece of sorrel, and I look for the male. Until I see him, I feel unsatisfied; something is incomplete. The bullfinch has an intense visual quality reminiscent of a Japanese print: its colours are sharply delineated, and its black cap, sitting low on the head over the eyes, merges with the fat black beak and chin in a dense opacity. But I cannot simply enjoy the gouache colours of these plump finches against the snow. The sight of a female bullfinch always triggers an anticipation of seeing the male: it is he who defines the species. Granted, with bullfinches, where you see one, you will usually see the other during most of the year except the nesting season, but my reaction holds true for all other birds, too. And there are worse effects. When I say 'I saw a bullfinch', I mean that I saw a male bullfinch. Unless I specify that it was female, it was male. I'm not alone in that. In casual conversation and in informal reports of sightings, the sex of a bird is almost only ever mentioned if it is female; the unqualified name means it is male – and that qualification acts as a detraction from its interest. If I read on a local bird blog that a female snow bunting has been seen out at the coast near Llanrhystud, or I watch a female hen harrier quartering the peat bog near Tregaron, I have the sense that it is of lesser importance, that it is not as exciting – even that there is something inconclusive about the sighting. It is the male who delivers the pleasurable sense of a definitive sighting of a species, and it is not difficult to see how this has come about.

By extension, it's no surprise, I suppose, that I find it difficult to see the equal value of my own life, or any woman's life, when viewed through such familiar and easily recognisable patterns. Those patterns, laid down so early on, were echoed and reinforced by representations of sexual difference every time I opened a bird book.

3. Mansplaining the Wild

Years after the announcement was made, I discovered that nature writing was finished – that it had been over since 2012. The obituary, written by a critic named Jim Hinch, appeared in the *LA Review of Books*. 'Nature writing is over', the headline declared. 'And Cheryl Strayed's *Eat, Pray, Love*-style autobiography *Wild* may have rung the genre's death knell.'

Apparently the genre doesn't know it's finished. Nature writing (though perhaps not what Jim Hinch would call nature writing) has shown no sign of decline. Nature as cure, nature as a playground, nature for extreme sport; nature as spectacle or escape or spiritual reset; nature as being there for us (purifying, humbling), or nature as being there for itself (autonomous, free of human contamination) – whether it's a metaphor or itself, books on the subject seem to proliferate like a species without a predator.

Jim Hinch didn't mean all nature writing, though.

He meant pure nature writing, the proper form, not the many bastardised derivatives such as the nature memoir, which signal its apparent decline. According to the evidence of book sales, the nature memoir is a wildly popular genre, but according to critics like Hinch, it's insufficiently wild. Strayed's *Wild* and subsequently Helen Macdonald's *H is for Hawk* have been blamed for that domestication. 'Far from reviving nature writing, *Wild*'s runaway success marks a further step toward extinction for the genre,' Hinch complains. 'However sophisticated recent memoirs have become... the genre is by definition human-centred and inward looking. Nature writing in its purest form challenges both of those literary impulses.' The 'best' nature writing, in his determination, 'looks away from the human narrator and seeks ultimately to lose the writerly self in a natural world both incomprehensible by, and often hostile to, human perception.'

Long after I read Hinch's review, I found myself arguing in my head with its author. It would pick up at odd moments – when I was sinking in over my ankles in black peat at Cors Caron ('See, Mr Hinch, it's pretty comprehensibly wet,' I'd mutter), or when I walked out of the village and up onto the boggy common, where in spring at least one pair of curlews still nests, though I no longer hear them in the valley. Not grand landscapes, either of those – but they're still forms of wilderness, even if tightly bounded.

In much of Hinch's review of Strayed's book, and of the nature memoir in general, he is repudiating the many glowing, admiring responses to the work that seem, to him, to reinforce not just a limited view of the natural world, but a damaging one. It's telling, he remarks, that 'almost all recently published nature-related titles are centred around a dramatic human narrative, not a landscape.'

Up on the common I wonder about Hinch's idea of the primacy of landscape. The common is all upland bog and rough pasture, springs and peaty watercourses. The distant lumpiness of Pumlumon and its rather indeterminate foothills lie away to the northeast, usually in cloud. On a clear day you can see the more defined peak of Cadair Idris further off to the northwest; close by, across the valley to the west, the wind turbines turn on Mynydd Bach, where there are hares and wheatears. I wonder if it would be possible to tell a dramatic story of these places without a human narrative.

I mistrust the love of wild places, and ideas of the natural world. I mean my own love of wild places, of the idea of the wild, as much as anyone else's. But mostly other people's ideas of it. I particularly mistrust an approach to the natural world and wilderness as something transformative and spectacular, when it can just as often be squalid and mundane. When I say I mistrust those approaches and ideas, it's because I know what's going on when I myself take any of those attitudes. And I do take them – I take all of them.

What Hinch describes as the 'best' nature writing is the kind I trust least. It has about it an absolute knowledge that I find alienating. If the authors consult field guides to help with identification, they don't let on. They name what they observe with unhesitating certainty. They don't describe some strange little fern or white-rumped sandy bird, and recount how they went home and found *spleenwort* or *female wheatear* in a field guide. Most of us can recognise and name only a tiny subset of what there is to identify, but nature writers appear to know these things preternaturally. The same is true of many of their critics, including Hinch; he doesn't seem to hesitate, or wonder about his own preferences, but states boldly what the natural order of things is or ought to be.

His review of *Wild* keeps coming back to me, like an old mosquito bite I've reignited by scratching. At first it is the whiff of denigrating women's experience that aggravates me. The nature memoir is the only area in the natural history of the world in which women predominate, and authors like Strayed, and more recently Helen Macdonald, have received an enviable amount of press and popular attention. It's Hinch's use of 'plucky young woman' to describe Strayed that is really suggestive, and galling. Like 'feisty' or 'strong', the implication in its use is that women are by default timid and weak, unless qualified by such an adjective. No one would describe a male writer as plucky (or feisty, or as a strong man, unless, in the latter case, he was a muscle-bound thug or dictator).

I can't help scratching at the irritation of Hinch's criticism. In his view, it's not just erasure of self that the best nature writers go into the wilderness to seek out; it is also to encounter 'nature's ultimate, grand indifference to human affairs'. Many people, I think resentfully, maybe even nearly half of humanity, spend their whole lives struggling against indifference and erasure, and erasure's ultimate expression, annihilation. Sometimes, therefore, might what some women seek in wilderness be a space in which we can return to ourselves, rather than a place in which we have to experience hostility and indifference? After all, we don't really need to be reminded that we don't matter, that we don't count. The patterns are instilled early, like the patterns in the field guides. *Maybe we don't need to seek erasure of self, Mr Hinch*, I think angrily; *maybe we need to seek respite from being erased by attitudes like yours.*

But that's not the only element in this aggravation. I am reacting, also, to a suggestion – or an inference on my part, at least – about what is the proper response to an experience of wilderness. I realise that the author has become a stand-in for my resentment of all the pointing men who've gone before him, men who, without authority and without being asked, have presumed to tell me where to look, and what to look at, and how to look.

Not all men, of course – but usually men. I remember a warm May evening a few years ago, when I drove with my friend John up to a bit of clear-cut ground near the Dyfi estuary to listen for nightjars. Clouds of midges were rising from the standing water and they enveloped us, biting us microscopically on the face, the hairline, the wrists. The itching agitated me, and I slapped at them ineffectually. The midges were everywhere, insinuating and voracious.

I'd never seen a nightjar, but the moment I heard the unmistakable churring sound, the midges were forgotten. John and I were instantly alert, looking at each other in the deepening dusk, delighted, and then looking around, straining to see the source of the sound. But the source of the sound was not a nightjar. It was a recording of a nightjar being broadcast from an MP3 player which a man was holding up as he walked towards us along the path with a group of people. He was bearded, dressed in a fisherman's vest and pale olive trousers with many useful pockets, and he was speaking authoritatively about nightjars, about how the recording would attract them. 'Welcome,' he said to us as he approached, claiming the space as his. He was well-meaning and enthusiastic, and I hated him. I wanted to set all the midges on him and then push him into the sullen water.

We got as far away from him as possible, and stopped again to listen, silently slapping at our necks, hunched against the itch, waiting and hoping. Then we heard the churring near us, and caught a glimpse of the dark bird with its strangely floppy, long-winged flight.

'Did you see it?' the helpful birdwatcher asked as we passed him on our way back. 'Yes, we saw it,' John said quellingly, and I thought, angrily, *we would have seen it without your help, thanks*, though I don't know whether it would have shown itself, or even called if it hadn't been for the man with the pockety trousers. When we were out of his hearing, John muttered grimly, 'I'm shaving off my beard.'

There's something innocent about them, the pointing helpful men: they are so caught up in their self-appointed expertise that they are unaware of how they conform to type. I met another of them, a memorable one, on Iona, off Mull, on a warm spring day in 2016. The ferry from Mull to Iona crosses a clear strait of brilliant turquoise, and when it docks, the disembarking passengers divide into two smooth slow-walking streams: the religious tourists turn right for the abbey and an encounter with the history of St Columba, and the birdwatchers turn left for the corncrakes. It was July weather when I was there, 27 degrees, though it was only April, but the infamous Scottish midges hadn't really started. A little along from the dock, a man in a pink pullover had set up a telescope in the tarmacked car park of the fire station. All the birdwatchers, including me, dutifully stopped to see what he was looking at. A sedge warbler was singing loudly, hidden in a gulley, but the man in the pink pullover showed us where to look, pointing at a patch of nettles in the field, where a brown bird was walking back and forth, enquiring for a mate with the raspy call of its Latin name, *Crex crex*. 'It's a male corncrake,' the man explained rather unnecessarily.

For me, the corncrake – like the now scarce nightjar and nightingale and turtle dove – belongs to the lost hazy childhood summers of previous generations in the nostalgic world of children's literature, when kids went off on bikes and drank ginger beer and caught swarthy bad guys. But even in Enid Blyton's racist rural landscapes of the 1940s, by which I was shaped in the 1970s, the range of the corncrake was already shrinking. In the 1941 *Handbook of British Birds* the distribution map for the corncrake includes the whole of the British Isles, but the text tells a story of the bird 'breeding regularly but in decreasing numbers' in northern England, and parts of Wales – 'Flint, Denbigh, Carnarvon, Anglesey and Pembroke'. Now, in the twenty-first century, the only place you are likely to hear or see a corncrake is the far northwest of the Scottish mainland, and some of the islands, including Iona.

I escaped the self-appointed expert and headed for the far side of the island, where bright eiders in breeding plumage were dabbling idly near the shore. Everywhere along the way, in the field edges, I heard *crex-crex, crex-crex*, that unmistakeable and now largely unknown summer sound like your nail along the teeth of a comb. But forever interposed between me and the first corncrake I'd ever seen was the pointing man in the pink pullover.

I can't hold Jim Hinch accountable for that man

in the pink pullover, or the many other men who have placed themselves, uninvited, between me and my experience of the natural world. And yet he fits seamlessly into the line-up, reinforcing my prejudices, because he assumes – as those other men have done – an authority and authoritativeness that is not earned. What grates particularly in his case is not just that quality of unselfconscious certainty about being right; it is also his presentation of an attitude as being universally true, when it seems to me as tenuous and problematic as the one he denigrates.

In contrast to the insufficiently wild (if admirably plucky) author of *Wild*, there's one writer, according to Hinch, who does take the right approach, and that is Robert Macfarlane, whom he describes as 'the current dean of world nature writing'. Macfarlane's book, *The Wild Places*, is, for Hinch, a 'superb 2008 travelogue of remnant wild places in the British Isles'.

Kathleen Jamie is less certain about Macfarlane's take on encountering the wild. 'What's that coming over the hill?' she asks in the *London Review of Books*. 'A white, middle-class Englishman! A Lone Enraptured Male! From Cambridge! Here to boldly go, "discovering", then quelling our harsh and lovely and sometimes difficult land with his civilised lyrical words.' She is not as beguiled as Hinch by Macfarlane's writing, which she sees as a continuation of an early monastic search for 'remote' places for 'some spiritual quest'. That monastic spiritual quest began a literary tradition which, she proposes, 'has persisted ever since and remains largely uninterrogated: the association of literature, remoteness, wildness and spiritually uplifted men.'

What Hinch presents as the ideal of nature writing, Kathleen Jamie identifies as self-involved. 'There are empty places, hill and moor and island out there, where, if you're minded,' she observes acerbically, 'you can meet no one else for a while, see nothing "intrusive" and have all the challenging, solipsistic experiences you please.' But, she points out, there are other ways of seeing those places – ways that don't unpeople them, or strip them of the history that shaped them, and that don't pass over the small and very local wild in favour of something on a grand scale.

Yes, precisely, I think, with more than a touch of glee. I wonder, a little viciously, whether Mr Hinch has ever killed a wasp, whether he would recognise being bothered by a wasp as an encounter with 'a natural world both incomprehensible by, and often hostile to, human perception'. Perhaps that apprehension of the natural world only works on the grand, spiritual scale of escape from self and from unwelcome humanity.

Perhaps it requires a spectacular landscape, while the local and familiar – and small, common species – do not count, because they do not deliver the same heady experience.

In the end of course I have to confront what is really irritating me: my argument with Jim Hinch is an argument with myself. Annoyingly, I recognise the shadow of my own attitudes in his. I, too, carry in me unexamined notions about the purity and autonomy of the natural world. I am shaped by the same cultural values into an exclamatory response to wilderness on a grand scale. And I am so much subject to the long reach of Romantic ideas of mountains that I cannot see mountains any other way. The very word mountain – or Mountain – is a stand-in for indifference to human experience. All the worst clichés pertain for me, and demonstrate just how clichés operate: not their problem of unoriginal description, but their problem of expressing familiar concepts, perceptions and experiences that are dulled and limited by generalisation. Hinch's view of transforming, erasing wilderness is one such cliché, and it's a clichéd perception that I share.

Nothing is more unwelcome in my experience of wilderness or wildness (or what I imagine is wilderness or wildness) than other people. Without them, I can ignore the fact that, in Western terms, wildness is only really wild if it is unobserved by a human. The purity of an encounter with the non-human animate world is contaminated by uninvited people, particularly if they don't approach it with the same respect for its sovereign otherness as I do – if they are noisy, or treat it as a playground, or a gym. Of course when I do the same things – if I go climbing, for example, all gear and guidebooks, or go birdwatching with binoculars – I don't do it like those others who are intruding on my empty wild landscape experience: I have the proper reverent, respectful attitude; I feel small and irrelevant and erased in the appropriate manner.

Uplifting and transformative, a humbling reminder of my insignificance – all of it is nonsense and culturally determined, even if, experientially, it's real and true. This apprehension of wilderness has very little to do with the erasure of self, the reminder of the world's indifference, or an annihilating encounter with the sovereign otherness of the natural world – or, rather, it only has something to do with these things because of how I am primed by my class and cultural training to experience the natural world this way, a training that includes, of course, any nature writing ('pure' or otherwise) that I have read.

The companion to this conventional response is the sense that this response is somehow *moral*. It leads to an insidious if unexpressed belief that moral attitudes and ethical behaviours inevitably result from it – attitudes and behaviours that include having a more humbled sense of what it is to be human; having a greater care of the non-human living world, and engaging more with its predicament. But the corollary to that belief is that a different response to the natural world leads to unethical – or at least irresponsible – behaviour.

Neither response is morally better, or moral at all. The conditioned Romantic response does not inevitably lead to trying to undo the catastrophe we've inflicted as a species, any more than a human-centred response to the natural world leads away from taking such responsibility. The former might result in anguish about the state of the natural world, but anguish, like guilt, only tells me that I care: it doesn't necessarily make me act. More often, the predicament of the natural world leaves me feeling paralysed, or, at best, full of nostalgia, or full of nostalgia's extinction-related relative, solastalgia.

The conditioned Romantic response to wilderness is a form of snobbery, a moral snobbery that extends to what constitutes valuable wildness or wilderness, too. None of that class and cultural training primes me to respond to bog the way that I am primed to respond, with heightened sensibility, to mountains, or sea cliffs and crashing waves. An osprey emerging from mist above the river, or a lone fox in the frost on Mynydd Bach? That's an encounter with wildness. But a man in a pink pullover pointing at a corncrake on Iona? It's not quite the same experience. Other humans sharing the encounter ruins its potential, and makes it mundane, even squalid. And what about the experience of trudging through the wilderness of endless upland blanket bog that constitutes so much mountain landscape? Yes, it erases, but not in an uplifting way; mostly it's exhausting to navigate, and makes me look forward to getting home.

That's how I feel reading a great deal of nature writing. All that relentless naming and authoritativeness and certainty is a hard slog through blanket bog, and I want to be done. I know how tenuous those certainties are in me, and so, perhaps unfairly, I mistrust them in others. I'd trust an account of the author trying and failing to definitively identify a beetle or a wildflower or a kind of rock, or getting it wrong, but uncertainty and inaccuracy don't make for much fine feeling, or much of an account at all.

One time, certain and authoritative, I got it badly wrong. Back in 1995, the man I lived with showed me a poem he'd written about his stepmother, who'd recently died. We'd gone to her funeral, up near Santa Rosa, in a rural area very different from the urban grit of Oakland, where we then lived. The poem was about a field of corn, a flock of crows rustling. After I'd read it, I handed the poem back to him. 'Crows don't flock,' I said, with condescending, self-appointed bird authority.

It's some twenty-five years since I made that insensitive birdsplaining mistake, and I will never forget his look of bewilderment and disbelief, and then hurt, and then anger. The poem, of course, was not about crows, but grief; he had not asked for my ornithological knowledge, and anyway my purported ornithological knowledge, given out with breezy certainty, was quite wrong, because American crows *do* flock.

When I found that out I wanted immediately to undo what I had said, but I could not acknowledge that I had got it wrong – about the poem, about crows, about the appropriate way to respond to his grief. Birds were the one thing I was certain I knew more about than he did; bird knowledge was my one area of expertise, and I could not face the damage to my pride.

And I was not only wrong about American crows:

I seem to have been wrong about crows in general. Eurasian crows can also flock. As a child I learned that they didn't, while rooks did. At a distance, this was the most obvious distinguishing feature between the two species. At least one of my childhood bird books from the 1970s reiterates it; so does Mark Cocker in his celebrated work, *Crow Country*. 'A carrion crow has a binding social attachment only to its mirror image, its partner,' he writes. 'It passes its life as one of a pair isolated from neighbours by a fierce territoriality. The largest congregation one normally encounters of the species is a late-summer band, involving two parents with a handful of offspring.' Perhaps that's true in East Anglia, the location of much of Cocker's account, and maybe it was true in south-east England where I grew up. Perhaps it had been observed in England, and universalised, with authority, for all of Britain. But in upland Ceredigion, where the land can support sheep but not crops, crows do indeed seem to flock in winter. Every time I walk under the rustling, clamorous opinions of some thirty carrion crows in a stand of bare beeches on the road towards Swyddffynnon, it surprises me as an anomaly, and then I remember my mistake.

But perhaps crow behaviour is changing; perhaps the whole family of corvids is changing and adapting.

There are ravens over the village now, all the time, when twenty years ago I would only hear or see them occasionally on the uplands of Mynydd Bach. In the overgrown thorn hedges marking field boundaries near the common I've seen groups of twenty or thirty magpies, which also aren't supposed to flock. Maybe these are young unmated birds, roving teenage gangs – but they are too numerous to be a family group. Perhaps the word 'flock' is the problem. No doubt ornithologists are more precise and discriminating about the group behaviour of birds, while I don't know the fine distinctions. Maybe I'm even mistaken about the crows: though I've checked carefully and double-checked, perhaps they are, after all, groups of young rooks that don't yet have the distinguishing bare base to their beaks or their baggy trousers (but then where are the adult rooks? I never see them there, and I know of no rookery anywhere nearby).

So it's not strictly true that I mostly mistrust others' ideas about wilderness, and the wild. The truth is that I mostly mistrust my own. And yet this leads to just the kind of approach that I object to in others: I think that because an encounter with the natural world elicits uncertainty in me, uncertainty is the only proper way to apprehend it – uncertainty about what we think we know, and what we can know. But much as I find unearned authoritativeness objectionable, I suppose uncertainty, too, can be a way of avoiding having to admit to getting things wrong, with all the embarrassment, and sometimes regret, which that entails.

4. Boggy Ground

It is 6.30 in the morning at Cors Caron, early in the spring, and I hope I might see an otter, or hear newly arrived warblers. Here the Teifi is still a narrow river running through peat bog, not many miles from its source. It has a long way to go before it reaches the Irish Sea at Aberteifi, but in spate it is already forceful. Cors Caron, a network of bog and waterways, of rough pasturage and drained field, serves as the river's floodplain. There are horses grazing in the reserve, and farms all around its edges, but its wildlife is rich and diverse.

A pair of goosanders lift from the river and take off upstream, and then a pair of mallards splatter off after them. I wonder if the goosanders are mergansers; I can never remember which of the two is coastal, which inland. A single pale buzzard skims low and suggestively as though it could be a female hen harrier.

I want it to be a harrier, but they've gone back north after the winter.

It is early, and still, and I need the toilet. I have come out before breakfast, and now the detritus from yesterday's meals is pressing upon me heavily and beginning to take up my attention.

On the far bank of the river, hidden in pale, tussocky grass, a small bird begins to call quietly, with a single repeated note. I have no idea what it is. I can't be bothered to stop and wait to see if it will show itself, flying from one perch to another. Further on, a reed bunting is calling, its white collar and black head visible above the reeds. I decide the first bird was a reed bunting too. I decide every small streaky thing I see is a reed bunting unless it is a pipit or a lark. The larks are just beginning. They launch themselves from me and climb away into the overcast early morning sky, and begin singing madly, as if the danger with which I present them has been a trigger. If it were summer, and the lark song was falling from a deep blue sky, all the romance of association might kick in, the detritus of literary ideas about larks. But it is cool and still and grey, as if waiting, and the larks are not an exultant wild but merely background noise to my increasingly pressing bodily need.

Soon, I am paying little attention to the buntings

or larks on the ground or in brief low flight. I am no longer interested in the irritation of identification. I can hardly tell a lark from a bunting, the urgency of finding a toilet is becoming so great. My intestines press insistently upon my consciousness and I no longer care that I have found the buzzard's feeding site. There are streaks of dark blood and small gobbets on the path-marker post, white splashes where the buzzard has lifted its tail and squirted *mutes*, that falconer's word for hawk shit which I know from TH White's *The Goshawk*, or possibly his *The Once and Future King*. I think of Robin Williams' mad character on his quest for the Holy Grail in *The Fisher King* – of the scene in which he recounts his moment of revelation while having 'one of those mystical shits', and I wonder what mystical experience lies ahead for me.

So far, the force of embarrassment has the upper hand over the force of my intestines. All around me the bog spreads out flat and open, unrelieved by cover, and the river is high, near the top of its banks. The bog seems empty of people, and the only house is a long way off, up on a slope among trees, but it's prime birdwatching territory, and an ideal time for someone to catch a glimpse of me with their binoculars. There is nowhere to get out of sight, no way to do the civilised thing of crapping unobserved.

Perhaps I should not be so concerned about propriety. Cors Caron is not, after all, a civilised place. On the contrary, it's primeval. That, at least, was its designation a century or so ago, when the Anglo-Jewish naturalist Charles Rothschild established the Society for the Promotion of Nature Reserves, and included 'The Tregaron Bog' in his list of proposed sites in 1915. It was a Reverend Owen, a vicar in Llandovery, who proposed the bog, sending in a survey form and map in response to the Society's invitation to the public to suggest areas that might be considered. The records of those proposals were digitised and published online in 2015, when the Wildlife Trusts marked the centenary of the publication of 'Rothschild's List', which comprised 284 sites.

The Society's survey form asked whether the proposed area was 'worthy of preservation as a piece of typical primeval country', to which Reverend Owen replied simply 'yes'. Was there any potential availability of local financial support 'should it be considered desirable to acquire the area'? asked the form. 'Doubtful,' he had replied. Was it 'locally popular as a pleasure resort?' 'No,' he wrote.

'The Tregaron Bog' is marked with a red cross on the area map that accompanies the vicar's survey form. The map shows a landscape of farms, smallholdings, single dwellings, and clusters around chapels. The two county towns, Tregaron and Aberystwyth, lie just beyond its bounds to the south and the northwest, making the bog appear rather more remote from population centres than it was. Near the northern limit of the map, in the village where I live, the Afon Wyre crosses the road as a ford, which is now a bridge; at the time there was a working mill and millpond, which is now only remembered in the building's old name, Yr Hen Felin, recently changed by a new owner into its English translation. Among the wind turbines on Mynydd Bach to the west lie the ruins of a lead-mining settlement, but on the vicar's survey map the settlement on the uplands appears to be intact.

A hundred years ago, perhaps my house, a smallholding dating back to the eighteenth century, would have seemed primeval to Owen, and to Rothschild, like many of the farms and smallholdings near Cors Caron – places in which people died of consumption and tetanus, of diphtheria and smallpox. No doubt there were fleas in the thatch, and the whitewashed walls were black with smoke. But though to Rothschild 'primeval' might have meant unchanged, uncivilised – in a word, *wild* – this rural hinterland had been shaped and tamed by human endeavour for centuries. Now there are walkways across the bog, and bird hides, and public paths and bold signage (and, about two long miles from me, a toilet). Then Cors Caron had peat-cutters, and the Manchester and Milford Railway, which was laid across the boggier parts on bales of sheep wool. A man in his eighties who has lived his whole life at its edge remembers how the surface of the water in the old peat cuttings used to tremble with the vibration of an approaching train long before the train could be heard.

The old railway line, now a public track, accompanies the road towards Pontrhydfendigaid, with its ruined Cistercian abbey, and then curves away from traffic and sets out in a straight line towards Ystrad Meurig, as though it is following the course of a Roman road. I encountered an adder here one September day, a large one, moving slowly. There was a wound across its head; it seemed confused, not seeking cover or escape. I wondered what it had fought itself free from – a weasel, perhaps, who had taken on a bit more than she had bargained for.

I leave the river with its indeterminate buntings and larks and pipits, and set off across the timber walkway towards the railway line. The walkway is tilting dangerously in places, and slats are missing; it requires continual repair to keep it from slipping into the bog. Nearby, preserved in peat, there are probably the bodies of those who set out and did not arrive. They'll never be found now that peat-cutting is finished here. The Iron Age bodies that have turned up in peat bogs in Ireland and Denmark, and Lindow Moss in England, have often been accidentally dismembered by peat cutters. Lindow Man – or what's left of him: his upper half and one leg – lies awkwardly displayed in a glass case in the British Museum. Only one find is on record for Cors Caron: a body without a head discovered by peat-cutters in 1811.

Like other peat bogs shaped by human labour, Cors Caron doesn't lend itself to Romantic understandings of what 'wild' means, either old or new. It's empty of people this morning, except for me, but only by effort could you unpeople its past and present, and apprehend it as primeval. But though it has been changed by humans, and, a century on from Rothschild's list, is domesticated as a reserve, the bog is still a place of wild encounter, even if that is sometimes only an encounter with unidentifiable pipits and buzzard shit – and, in my case, the erasing, uncivilised aggravation of my body's wild needs.

5. Curious Bodies

Ahead of me, in a patch of sunlight, there is something lying on the crumbling tarmac. The road downhill is mossy, shady and damp under overhanging trees, but there's a gap where the sun has broken through the leaves. As I approach, a buzzard flies off from a tall ash, and now I can see what's lying ahead of me: it's the lower part of a sheep's leg – about twelve inches of leg, and the black hoof. It is dry, clean, with no blood, no smell, not until I bend down at least, and then it gives off only the scent of warm wool, of sheep in sunshine.

Kathleen Jamie or Mary Oliver, happening on a sheep's leg in the road, would be curious, and they'd bring it home, and later they would write about it: coolly, impersonally, making some larger observation – about death, obviously; perhaps about endings. There's Kathleen Jamie's account of boiling a gannet's skull, Mary Oliver finding a fox carcass.

It's autumn, but like summer – an Indian summer,

I think, recalling California at Halloween, acres of pumpkins under a hot sky in empty lots off the freeway, acorn woodpeckers at Point Reyes drilling holes to keep their winter stores, and Jaime De Angulo's Fox Boy and Bear walking in Bay Area fog, Old Man Coyote telling them the story about Weasel, who set fire to the world because he was mad.

This autumn it's been eighteen degrees each day – cool at night, beginning to be cold near dawn, but not yet frosty. The sycamore leaves have dried and started to curl. It is quiet here under the trees: just the buzzard off in the distance, with its derisive cry, and the stream, running from high up on Mynydd Bach, where it's dug a mossy gully by the ruined farmhouse, down to its confluence with the Afon Wyre in the valley below me.

Sometimes I wish this boggy upland conformed more closely to a pastoral ideal – Hardy's, say, where field names suggest deep history; ancient stone barns stand unchanged for generations, and the boundaries are marked by tidy, traditionally laid hedges – or even the pastoral poems that hanker after Hardy, in which the land is dotted with clean white sheep whose lambs slip out like minnows in moonlight. There aren't bits of carcass like this in the celebrated pastoral poems, and the pastoral world the poems hanker after. There are no rags of black silage plastic caught in those hedges or clogging the ditches; no rotten fences stopped up with fraying orange baling twine; no rusting barbed wire trailing in the mud, threatening tetanus. Sheep in those poems don't limp or graze kneeling because both front hooves are rotten. There is no hoof rot, no botfly, no flystrike, where maggots burrow into a ewe's flesh.

But this boggy country is not a pastoral poem. Here the walls have long since fallen, and rags of black plastic flap on the barbed wire. The sheep, crowded into a churned field for the tupping season, are caked under their tail and down their legs.

In my pocket I have a bag for mushrooms, though they are scarce this autumn, and there's no smell of them even in the damp banks here either side of the road. Stooping down, I turn the bag inside out over the leg as if I were a diligent dog owner picking up a hot turd. I look behind me before I do it, and afterwards, to make sure no one has seen me. I am afraid that it is improper, and that it might be illegal, and as I walk home with my illicit find, some fleeting notion of foot-and-mouth, of mad cow disease, of the disposal of fallen stock, passes through my mind.

I leave the bag with the sheep's leg on the rusting milk churn inside the gate: I cannot bring myself to examine it, but I am intent on bringing myself to examine it. I've brought it home, after all, so now I need to see it through – now I need to decide what to do with it. And what would I say if someone were to ask me what I was doing – that I was simply curious? Curious about what, exactly? I am not yet sure.

My thoughts circle around the ewe's leg and away, for even lifting it and carrying it in a bag and bringing it home is the breaking of a taboo. What am I going to do with it? And what am I going to do when I have finished with it? When I have watched it change, and begin to smell and decay, I will have to get rid of it.

I think of the deer that I saw shot, disembowelled and dismembered back in February, when I'd asked a conservation organisation if I could come along to observe their deer culling. They'd said I was welcome to, but I was warned by Sarah, one of the officers who managed land on Skye, that it would be a hard slog. She described how, without a predator, deer proliferate, and they strip the land. Unlike the deer stalking of game estates, the purpose of conservation culling is to restore some balance in an ecosystem that is wildly out of balance. We were outside the stag season, she said, so they'd be culling hinds instead.

She was right about it being hard going. Because of the direction of the wind we had to walk several miles along the valley floor below the snowy peaks of the Cuillin, before we could strike uphill and then make our way back along the ridge to get above the deer. Sarah and her fellow conservation officer, Ally, zig-zagged uphill quickly, following near invisible deer paths through straggled dead bracken stems and deep tripping heather. Ponderous as a carthorse, and noisier, I stumbled after them. The weather closed in, and when it began to rain we stopped to take shelter in a corrie, Ally and Sarah lying down and folding themselves in under the protection of a small overhang.

After it eased, we set off again, but when, finally, we reached the ridge, it began to snow wetly, and then it turned to stinging sleet. I followed their dark figures, bent over so that we would not show. Then, coming down off the ridge, we crawled on hands and knees through the snow, and finally worked our way on our stomachs a few inches at a time to an outcrop above the slope where the herd of deer were grazing below us, unaware. We stopped there, and Ally and Sarah slowly reached round behind for their rifles, and eased them into position. We waited, lying flat on our stomachs in the slushy heather. It was snowing again, wet snow, and with it there was a blanketing silence now that we were out of the wind on the ridge. There was not so much as a raven – only the deer below us.

It seemed a long time before the first shot, followed immediately by the second. Two animals dropped, fell from sight, and the rest sprang away, bounding quickly out of range.

Sarah got bloodied to the elbows, gralloching the hind. Above us, the peaks of the Cuillin had retreated into cloud. It was silent there at the bottom of the slope where the deer lay on her back, disembowelled, and the entrails steamed in the cold air. Sarah cut out the heart and tossed it into the heather, and the kidneys, heavy and round. She pulled out the collapsed lungs, a pale frothy membrane. A final pellet fell from under the hind's tail, as though even after death and dismemberment the body's inner processes were continuing. But there were no longer any insides.

The kidneys were springily resistant to the touch, and the lungs had a strange and alien texture, both foamy and substantial. In my hand the hot heart lay heavily, the size of a human heart – neither symbol nor quite an organ, but bloody chambered muscle. I wondered how you could eat a thing like that, with all its rubbery tubes. Steam was rising from the stretched white bags of the stomachs, and Sarah nicked them and peeled back a small flap, so I could see the stages of digested and semi-digested food: in the first, a rough green mulch; in the second a green mush, like pesto.

Sarah had been trained by Ally, who was making quick work of the second animal further down the slope. She was still learning. Gralloching a pregnant hind was difficult, she said – that was more challenging. But otherwise she was used to it. She didn't think about it much. This one that she'd shot had fortunately not been pregnant.

The two hinds were small and bony. It had been wet for months, which took its toll more than a hard winter, Sarah said, because being wet meant being always cold, and the deer, less able to compete for scarce food, succumbed more easily to illness and starvation.

After she'd gralloched the hind, she broke its back legs, and cut off their lower half. Then she stuffed the hindquarters into a backpack and hoisted it onto her back. When we set off down the slope towards the valley bottom, we left behind the forequarters and entrails and organs – for the ravens and eagles, though we saw and heard no birds at all in that still, snowy mountainscape.

The day after I bring the sheep's leg home, it begins to smell in the unseasonable autumn sun. At last I take it out of the bag and lay it on a stone. It's a lower back leg, the foot bent at an angle, as if the ewe died standing with her weight on the tip of her hoof. I wonder where the rest of her lies, whether her carcass has been torn into and dismembered, a trail of dirty wool and entrails, or if she is lying tensely swollen, as though about to explode.

A dead badger lay like that earlier in the summer under the hedge on the road to Swyddffynnon, about a mile outside the village. It's narrow there, with high banks and dense fenced hedges of hawthorn and blackthorn; there is nowhere for a badger to escape if some driver comes upon it, if – vindictive, or just for the casual thrill – instead of slowing, he speeds up. Or perhaps it was an accident, someone going fast late at night on the empty road; perhaps it had been killed elsewhere and dumped there. I walked or ran that way most days, holding my breath as I approached it and passed it and for a good bit beyond it, depending on the direction and strength of the wind.

Soon after its death, the body began to swell. Over days it became so distended with gas I thought it must burst. I began to speed up to get past it, afraid I might witness or even be spattered by the nightmare moment of its rupture.

The badger's tough skin, an effective barrier to predators while alive and to scavengers when dead, seemed able to accommodate enormous swelling pressure from the gas given off by internal decomposition; it appeared impenetrable. No kite or crow opened up the carcass. It remained intact, ballooned and tensely horrible, about to give at any moment. And then, intact, it began to shrink. Day after day it collapsed and dried. The smell faded. Soon after, the corpse flattened and began to come apart. Perhaps now carrion birds got to it; perhaps kites scavenged it, but I never saw a bird rising from it at my approach – never saw a magpie or crow or kite anywhere near it. It began to shed fur, to break up. One day I found ribs, limbs, teeth scattered along the verge. There remained only a faint occasional whiff of corruption, close to, and I stopped running past it, and instead slowed and stayed and examined the parts: the long wavy multicoloured hairs, the curved claws.

Ewes don't rot down intact, like badgers. Instead they become flesh, torn into at all their vulnerable places by ravens, if higher up, or by magpies or crows which hop springily away when you come near, and sidle back when you've gone past. I wonder where they began with this ewe, after the eyes.

Earlier, in the spring, at the edge of the trees along the stream near where I found the leg, I saw a lamb that had been blinded by a feasting magpie or crow.

Its empty eye sockets had bled profusely before it died; its face was a red raccoon mask. It's a common enough sight in spring anywhere there are new weak lambs and the corvids that keep them company, but it's never something I can get used to. I think each time of the boy in Niall Griffiths' *Sheepshagger*, who pushes pebbles into a living lamb's bloody eye sockets.

My neighbour was fencing with a young man by the road and I mentioned the lamb, under the beeches, that it had been there two days, and he looked up rheumy eyed, bent, bulky, and said 'So fe'n perthyn i fi' – disclaiming ownership, and therefore interest, or action.

On the second day the leg begins to leak, and the flies come and busy themselves at the moist places. There is a fluid around the bone, and the black keratin of the hoof and the knob of fetlock deepens to a rich tacky sulphur. The flies jostle, glossy and iridescent, all eagerness for the smell and what it promises. At first it is just the same dense oily smell that lingers in the wake of a passing sheep trailer packed with fattened lambs, their faces pressed up against the slats, on the way to slaughter down at the abattoir in Llanybydder. The hot smell as they pass takes a long time to dissipate – a smell of liquid dung and urine and hooves and oily wool.

At first this is the smell the leg gives off. And then the flesh begins to rot. I try to analyse the smell, what it constitutes, how it seems less a smell than a coating on the air – the smell of decomposing flesh that is so unlike other smells of decomposition. It is only a gas, or a medley of gases given off, I suppose, by bacteria multiplying, exuding toxins that break down large and small and microscopic structures, of tissue and cells and molecules – and yet it clings to the air like a substance, like an oil, as though it is heavier than gas. It coats my mouth, my nose, so that I feel covered in it. Hours later I smell it, or I imagine I smell it, as though the contamination is sustained far beyond its source, but it is only the physical echo of the smell that stays, somehow, in my senses. If I reach after the scent of gorse, or haymaking, I can capture a hint, the memory of a scent, but the smell of decay clings, like a smear of dog shit that you can't get off your shoe. It does not move into memory, from which, remembering, I retrieve it, but instead remains alive, physical and present, long after I am far from its origin.

The deer's entrails had not smelled, but the entrails of domestic animals reek. It's the guts that cause the stench outside an abattoir; it's the guts that go off fast. The writer Cynan Jones told me about the time a slaughterhouse container had been parked for days in exceptional summer heat by the sea in Aberaeron – how the expanding gases from the decomposing entrails made the container explode, and how the sudden stink caused people to vomit in the street. I had turned away from him, repelled; I returned to it and flinched from it, and from him, as though he was contaminated, and would contaminate me. And it's the smell that stayed with me after I watched a hog slaughtered. A friend with a smallholding in Pembrokeshire had invited me, knowing I'd observed deer culling in Scotland. 'We'll be slaughtering our pigs in the autumn,' she'd said. 'You're welcome to come and watch.'

The slaughterman, Len, talked in a quiet intimate final conversation with the hog, holding an apple in his hand for it to eat. He was gentle with the bolt gun, holding it to the hog's head for a still moment. It was important, he said later, that the animal not be stressed: it changed the meat.

After the hog dropped, the men tied a rope around its hock, dragged it up by a tractor hoist and cut its throat, catching the dark gouts of blood in a bucket as the body kicked and jerked and convulsed as if struggling to get free, though it was dead.

The men carried the carcass to the shed and laid it on a trestle table, following Len's instructions. With kettle after kettle of boiling water, he cleaned and scraped the hide, then cut off the head, and in the rising steam and smell of hot skin, he and one of the men hooked and hauled the carcass towards the shed ceiling, and Len cut it open in one swift swipe down from the throat.

The intestines spilled out of the slit belly and hung there for a moment, intact. The small intestine, purple, delicate, was the colour of a faint bruise, the large intestine yellow-ochre. Len, delicate with the knife, nicked the final tissue and the whole lot came free. He flung the mass into a plastic bucket where it slopped, both liquid and substantial, with a great waft of moist clinging stench.

After the pig slaughter, the men talked fast and loudly over tea, about other slaughters, upping the ante on shock value. It might have been only adrenaline, but there was something frantic about their release. One of them told a story about a friend who'd left a ewe's entrails in a closed garage, and the windows turned metallic black with flies, the whole humming like a power station. I started out on the horror story of the trailer of entrails in Aberaeron, but he interrupted, took over; he knew the story, and embellished it.

But Len, the Pembrokeshire slaughterman, with his white eyebrows and narrow face, listened in silence, ate sandwiches, cake, drained his mug of tea and held it out for a refill, and then quietly began a story about his sharpening steel, which he'd bought in New York City for $25. He was a practised raconteur, one of those storytellers who, once launched, is unable to deviate from the unfolding narrative, which he'd told many times – and for whom a conversation is less an exchange than a series of opportunities for a story. He had one about every implement he used. The steel would have cost £150 in the UK, he said. The man who sold it to him told him he obviously knew what he was looking at, and, at the conclusion of their conversation, said it had been wonderful, beautiful to hear him, 'to hear the old accent', and then said – Len paused, building towards the punchline – 'give my love to Donegal'. We laughed dutifully.

'Why do you need to actually witness what happens?' a poet asked me, when I told him about the pig slaughter, the deer culling. 'Isn't the power of imagination enough?' We were in a café, looking out over the sea, and his face showed fastidious distaste, though it was much more than distaste – it was revulsion at the subject, revulsion at me for my interest.

I remembered an event, years before, in an arts centre in Berkeley, when Thom Gunn had read some poems about the serial killer Jeffrey Dahmer from his new collection, *Boss Cupid*. The arts centre, which had a regular programme of well-attended poetry readings, stood in a leafy park in a wealthy neighbourhood, and the audience filling the seats was mostly grey haired. The poet, an English émigré who'd lived in San Francisco since 1954, was celebrated for his formal work and gay themes, particularly *The Man with Night Sweats*. But his poems about the AIDS epidemic of the 1980s had been easier to stomach than his new poems about Jeffrey Dahmer. They'd been part of an opera, he said, which, for some reason, hadn't got off the ground. Some members of the audience tittered dutifully, a little nervously, prepared to be open-minded, liberal. But Thom Gunn crossed a line. It wasn't the body parts and cannibalism that proved too much for many of them; they sat through those poems silently, faces tense with distaste and discomfort. But when he started to suggest that as humans we were all capable of terrible acts; that, under different circumstances, each of us could behave as horrifically and incomprehensibly as this serial killer, a cannibal, a necrophile, some members of the audience stood up and left, flushed and outraged, their revulsion at the suggestion turning into revulsion at him.

In the café overlooking the sea, watching as the poet gathered his belongings, his coat, and got up to leave, the feeling that I had been found repellent made me squirm inside, made me hot and unclean. I watched him hurry away, as though he feared contamination, and I regretted telling him, because now I felt ashamed of my curiosity.

We start with curiosity, as infants: as soon as we begin to gain control of our hands we try to explore the curious world with our fingers and our mouths. But we have to learn disgust. There are good reasons for it: disgust protects us from harm, from contamination and poisoning and contagion. Later it feels existential, as if it's an innate response to danger, but what tells us something is dangerously unclean is encultured taboo. Our social taboos about acceptable and repulsive curiosity are sexually dimorphic, too: 'Ugh, don't look, don't touch,' my mother would tell me, but to my brother she would only say 'Go and wash your hands.'

When I was nine, I found a dead fox in the exposed roots of an old blackthorn, where there was a rabbit warren. There were flies, but almost no smell. Perhaps it had eaten poisoned bait; perhaps there was no bait, and it had been injured or ill or old, and had lain down there and died. Mary Oliver, finding a dead fox curled in a tyre, in a posture 'of looking / to the last possible moment, // back into the world', has an epiphany: she touches the fox, and it vanishes, and it is she who is leaving the world instead. I did not touch the fox, but I kept going back to look at it, and each time it had shrunk a bit, wetly, and stank a bit more, and, when I looked closely, I found it had come alive with maggots. I was nine, and didn't have a spiritual epiphany. Instead I felt ashamed of my interest. I knew I was supposed to be disgusted – and I was. But I was curious too.

Stink and rot and maggots were an unremarkable part of the world I moved in then: my sister and I worked all weekend and every day during school holidays at a farm two miles away, mucking out and riding the horses, and helping with a flock of sheep and a herd of Highland cattle. The sheep of my childhood in south-east England were as unromantic as the limping maggot-ridden sheep of mid Wales. Hoof rot and flystrike were endemic there too, in the 1970s. Now the reality of flystrike fills me with a kind of horror: my insides squirm, appalled by the idea that flies, attracted to wet or shitty wool, or wounds, lay eggs that hatch maggots which burrow in, and feed, engorged, on a ewe's flesh – and pupate and emerge and lay in turn. But when I was a child it was unremarkable. In the summer, at the concrete dip, full of dark liquid, it was my job to lift the gate to let the sheep through, one at a time. Harry, the farmworker, grabbed them by the fleece and tossed them in when they hesitated, shouting, 'Get in there you old bugger.' Usually they came through the gate with such force that they leapt into the dip before they realised, and swam frantically, heads tilted back, just nose and eyes and ears above the surface, to the far end, where each was pushed under with a rod, to ensure they had been fully submerged before they heaved themselves out, their fleeces streaming.

Late in her life, my sister attributed her years suffering from chronic fatigue to the long after-effect of exposure to the organophosphates used in dipping sheep in the 1970s. But I remember the smell of creosote in the dip, and when the farmer treated flystrike in the field. Showers of maggots used to fall from a wound afterwards.

I don't know when I learned to feel disgust, but something about that memory of the fox that I kept returning to fills me with shame. Maybe I told someone about it, and the home it made to flies and eggs and maggots; maybe they reacted with disgust, recoiling from me with revulsion, as if I were contaminated, the way the poet recoiled from me as if I might contaminate him. Perhaps shame is the mechanism that drives home the lesson of disgust. Shame is what drove it home for me.

On the third day, the sheep's leg gives off a stench. After I go out and examine it, and flinch from the smell, I think I can smell it inside the house, though all the windows and doors are closed to keep out the heat. I wonder why I have brought it home instead of leaving it in the road for a scavenger; I have forgotten why I was curious, why I wanted to push against the voice that still tells me *Ugh, don't look, don't touch.* The leg sits outside on the milk churn, visited by flies, waiting for me to decide what to do. I have taken responsibility for it, so I can't return it to the place I found it, reinstating what I disturbed.

I look up Mary Oliver and discover there are two poems about dead foxes. In one, which recounts taking home a carcass, she recalls 'the building of glass and stone' where 'down the long aisles, and deep inside the drawers, are the bones of women and children, the bones of old warriors.... Mute, *catalogued*.' Then she reconsiders: 'I could see how it was, and where I was headed. I took what was left of the fox back to the pinewoods and buried it.'

I find that I've misremembered Kathleen Jamie too. She did cut off a gannet's head but, uncertain and inexperienced, she too had made a mistake: she put it in caustic soda to remove the feathers and flesh. 'Daily, I stirred the mess with a stick, but the gannet merely bobbed up to glare at me from the pot.... Eventually the bones didn't clean but softened, and the liquid turned a foul brown-green and, gagging, I tipped the lot into a hole in the flowerbed.'

I think of the culled hinds in the snow, gralloched and dismembered, and the stags, later in the year, in Sutherland, the far north, when I'd gone back to Scotland for the stag season. Like Sarah in Skye, Don, the land manager in Sutherland, warned me it would be a long trudge across blanket bog, and there was no guarantee we would come up with any deer. On the cluttered dashboard of his old Land Rover he had a well-worn paperback by Joy Harjo, the native American poet, though I don't recall which collection it was. Perhaps it was *A Map to the Next World*; perhaps it was *How We Became Human*. He read a poem from it before he opened the door and got out. He said he always read a poem of hers before he went stalking deer.

We set out across a treeless flat landscape. Occasionally he would stop to point out a black smear of otter spraint, or sundews, or brown hare droppings, but mostly we trudged in silence through tripping, tussocky, pathless blanket bog until we came upon recent signs of deer: fresh droppings, and deer flies. Then, a little further on, the smell of the stags came to us on the wind, hot and musky.

When we got close we dropped down and approached on hands and knees, and then Don gestured to me to get right down, and I crawled behind him on my stomach, my face close to the tough, woody little snakes of juniper growing flat to the ground. Don stopped behind a small rocky outcrop, and cautiously, slowly raised his head to look through a gap. Then he pulled back and gestured to me to take a look. Beyond the outcrop five hinds were grazing, with a calf and two stags.

Don shot the first stag, and the others took off – but then they slowed and turned back. They walked past in front of us in a line, a few metres away, heads up, mouths open and panting: alert, alarmed, but not terrified. Then Don shot the second stag, and the others leapt away and were gone.

By the time we got to the first stag its eye had dulled to a dark green with a pale sheen, like an unpolished gemstone, and two flies were already busy there and at the entry wound. Don's knife cut through the hide like a razor along the grain of sheer fabric, and he gralloched the stag swiftly. Oesophagus, intestines, heart, lungs, liver, stomachs all coalesced into a rounded, glistening mound. Using a thumb-covering of intestine, he pushed the last pellets of dung out from under the tail, onto the heather. 'Fewmets,' he said, and instantly I was back in TH White's *The Once and Future King* where the hapless King Pellinore keeps showing everyone the elusive Questing Beast's precious fewmets.

Don went off to fetch his ATV from the trailer, so he could take the two stags out, and while he was gone, two ravens passed by, checking things, but not yet approaching. Later, there was some quarrelling, and three of them gathered, alert to something, and then a golden eagle skimmed past just above the rim of the next valley. The rifle shots had brought them.

After we loaded the carcasses onto the ATV, fore and aft, and set out, we left behind two bulging mounds of entrails and organs, and the legs and antlered head of each stag, which Don had carefully placed, like an offering.

Remembering those cairns left for the scavenging ravens and eagles, and recalling my own scavenger, the buzzard that I'd put up from the sheep's leg, I regret what I have done. Some things can, after all, be left to the imagination, and there is also the matter of respect. I do not need to wait for the flies' work to come alive and hatch and get to work in their own way. Not everything needs to be observed, or experienced or known.

In the evening of the third day I go out and bury the sheep's leg by the woodshed.

6. Uninvited Guests

The plumber came to the top of the stairs and called down to me in the kitchen: 'I think you'd better come and see this.'

I put down the coffee pot and went upstairs. He was on the stepladder into the attic, where he was getting ready to replace the cold-water tank. 'You've had a visitor up here,' he said, and handed down the boards that serve as the attic trapdoor. In among some shreds of insulation, there was a lot of old dried scat, each piece about an inch and a half long, and twisty, ending in a point. Not a rat, then, which had been my first fear, nor a squirrel. The twisted shape and pointed end suggested carnivore to me, but what carnivore could get into my attic?

The house is built at one end into the rock, and the external wall is rough uneven sloping stone: it would be easy enough to climb up and get under the slates if you were small enough – a weasel, say, but the scat was too big for a weasel. A polecat, then, or a stoat, or possibly a mink – my neighbours across the road had seen a mink earlier in the year. The attic would surely be good hunting ground for any of them. I always have voles in the attic, and often house mice, and sometimes a wood mouse. Once, when I found a suggestively gnawed hazelnut shell in my bedroom, I thought I had a dormouse, but learned to my regret that the gnawing signature around the inner rim was that of a wood mouse.

I took the scat downstairs and found an online guide to British mammal shit (the Mammal Society's 'Whose poo?' was a useful starting point). It confirmed my guess: the twisty shape was carnivore; the particular twisty shape was that of mustelids, and the size was stoat or polecat. I would have loved it to have been a stoat, but I'd never seen one. I had seen a polecat, though, sauntering across my lawn at dusk, and on another occasion with kits near the Rheidol, and I see polecat roadkill all over mid Wales.

The polecat brought to eight the number of mammal species who have made my house their home – polecat, wood mouse, house mouse, bank vole, field vole, common shrew, pipistrelle bat, and me. Probably also at times there have been brown rats and grey squirrels and dormice; perhaps other species of bat;

perhaps a weasel also getting in under the slates, but not to my knowledge in the twenty years I've lived here. There was also a stray ewe who tried very hard to make it her home one spring morning when I'd left the back door open: she came in with her lamb, and I chased her round the living room, only just heading her off before she made a bid for the stairs, and my bedroom. Fifty years ago there would almost certainly have been orphaned bottle-fed lambs, and dogs, a cat; a century ago, probably cattle, their heat rising into the attic from the barn end of the house, when there was still a barn. There's only the mark, now, in the render of the talcen, but I know how it used to look, because a neighbour gave me a photograph of a painting that a friend of hers had done of the house, sometime back in the 1960s, before the barn was knocked down.

The plumber seemed bemused by my excited reaction to what he'd found, and I can see it might have been a bit odd. But mammal scat is like a gift left by a visitor who called while you were sleeping or were busy elsewhere. It's a sign that you share your space, that your management of what's outside your house – and on occasion, what's inside it – is hospitable (or, if you're otherwise inclined, a sign of your negligence).

Some people would be horrified by the feral way I live, but even if I tried, I could not keep my neighbours out. I live in a porous eighteenth-century traditional stone bwthyn. Its near-metre-thick exterior walls are rough stone, built in two skins that are pinned and filled with rubble, typical of the vernacular architecture of rural Wales. The pitched roof, built of pine rafters under slate, rests on black oak beams, and tongue-and-groove boards make up the interior walls and ceilings. The back door used to be warped, and on a windy day, the curtain drawn across it would billow into the room. The old single-glazed sash windows used to tremble and buzz with passing traffic, and in spring it was impossible to sleep beyond dawn because the birdsong was so loud.

Since I got the door and windows replaced, I have missed the immediacy of the dawn chorus, though not the loud noise of the passing traffic. But even with double glazing and a new tight-fitting door, my home is still full of entryways, the walls hollow with invisible tunnels, the attic undisturbed. My house is more access to shelter than barrier against incursion. It keeps the weather out, but lets in those seeking respite from weather. There are the mammals, and insects everywhere, visible and invisible, and their evidence (that of woodworm in particular).

In spring the solitary bees emerge from

hibernation, and come searching for nest sites in the south-facing wall. Some are mason bees, all orange fuzz; others are leaf-cutter bees, dark, with a bright orange belly, and there are still others that I have not identified. During mating, the pairs of bees, with the male clamped on like a small rider, become so absorbed by procreation that they drop to the ground and lie in a kind of torpor, oblivious and unresponsive.

In the sun, the female bees bump against the warming stone, trying to find old or new gaps in the lime mortar where each will hollow out spaces to lay her eggs. Most of them choose entry holes too high up the wall for me to look in, but later in the year, when the sun rises above the treeline and lights up the whole south side of the house, sometimes a bee will choose a crevice lower down. Then I watch her going in, and wait to see what she will do. Her dusty velvet bottom will reappear first as she reverses out, sealing up the tunnel as she goes. Sometimes a leaf-cutter bee will arrive with her circular section of leaf, but mostly the evidence that they are present is the sawn-out holes in the leaves of a nearby rose. After the bees lay an egg in each cell they have built, they back out and block up the hole, using some combination of saliva and leaf and mortar dust. The camouflage is so complete that, once a bee is finished, I cannot find the filled hole. But the tiny iridescent turquoise and red parasitic wasps must find some of them. They come later in the year, in the early summer, and scurry busily about on the wall, looking for a way in.

The first solitary bees arrived a few years ago, after I had the trees along the ridge to the west cut down, and the wall got direct sunlight during the afternoon. Now by late spring there are dozens bobbing and bumping their way in. There are so many that I thought for a while they were not solitary bees at all, but wild honey bees with a hive in the wall above my door. I wonder how it looks; I imagine some labyrinthine New York high-rise apartment complex in among the rubble in the wall cavity.

Though it's a home to mammals and insects, and occasionally amphibians and gastropods, no birds nest in any part of my house. The gable end is east-facing, the wrong direction for house martins, and the south-facing eaves are too low even for sparrows. One spring a redstart investigated the gutter, and a gap that had opened under a slipped slate. Instead she chose a hole in the wall of the ruined outbuilding, and laid a single blue egg, before she and her mate got seen off by the robins' persistent harassment.

But every spring, when the swallows return, I am faced with a dilemma: should I let them in? It begins almost as soon as they arrive. On a warm April day, if I leave the back door open, within minutes a swallow will be swooping around, checking it out. The exposed beams in my dark, barn-like living room offer just the kind of sheltered high flat space where swallows like to nest, and often a pair will sweep around the open door persistently, back and forth, circling round, hesitating, sliding away, and returning. When they've come in, I have always chased them out. But w*hat if...* I wonder every year. *What if I leave them alone? What if this one chooses to nest here? What if I let her?* Every spring I wait for their return; every spring, part of me wants that dark blue shimmer of hollow bone and stiff feather to take the risk. Each time I wonder about leaving a small window open, and giving over my living room to them. The floor is old quarry tile, and I'd cover the furniture. Their mess would do no damage; the mess, and the noise of nestlings, would only be an inconvenience for a few weeks.

In recent years there have been fewer and fewer swallows near my house, and there are fewer and fewer places available for them to nest. Barns are converted into holiday cottages, or knocked down to make way for chicken sheds; outbuildings are made into garages or garden offices or guest rooms. Entryways everywhere are being sealed off and blocked up or netted. But despite the loss of swallow nest sites year on year, every spring I shut my door to them.

I'm not sure inviting swallows to nest in your living room, or delighting in polecat shit in your attic, is quite what the RSPB meant when it urged people with its campaigning slogan to 'give nature a home'. Even allowing the natural world into your garden can be a challenge, if you're inclined towards swathes of dandelion-free golf-course lawn, mown and sprayed into shaven acquiescence; or cemented-over patios, surrounded by tight-fitting fences or brick walls that let nothing through; or violently weeded borders of low-maintenance, mess-free evergreen shrubs. To let go of a bit of control and allow the wild in might make a small difference, even though what we really should do for hedgehogs, according to hedgehog activist Hugh Warwick, is to 'dismantle industrial capitalism'. But no one suggests you should make your *house* a home for nature: that is a step too far. We might be asked to provide nest boxes and pollen-rich flowers to support wild things in our gardens, but we are expected to try to keep 'nature' out of our living space. To do otherwise is to step beyond the frontier of normal and acceptable human behaviour.

*

The wood beyond my garden is a wet slope of mature trees leading up to a fenced ridge. Beyond the fence, sheep graze acres of boggy upland field. No one is quite clear who is responsible for this wood, or for the fence that keeps the sheep out. The wood is left to itself, full of fallen trees and brambles clambering over rotting branches. It's loud with birdsong in spring and summer, and bright with bluebells in May. There are mature beeches and oaks and ashes along the ridge line; year after year the bark has swollen and grown around the wire where the fence is stapled to the trunks. The wire is rusty and easily broken, and when the sheep get through I hear them sounding too loud, so I pull on boots, a pair of work gloves, and clamber up the steep ridge, sliding in churned earth and leaf mulch, to chase them back into the field. Each time I plug the new gap as best I can – with rusty barbed wire and blackthorn, hard and vicious, but it's only ever a temporary measure.

There is no such fence between the wood and my garden: the line is marked only by the shaggy overgrown place where I arbitrarily decide to stop cutting brambles and grubbing up ash sprouts. In among the mature trees saplings grow tall and spindly in search of light, and by autumn there is always new hazel, hawthorn, sycamore and ash growing where previously there were only brambles. Occasionally I cut it back ruthlessly, but some years the wood creeps close to the house. Ash and sycamore seeds will scatter everywhere in the wind, and take root in the gutters, between roof slates. In a very short time, without control, the encroaching wood could be the undoing of my house.

Miles further west, beyond this strip of wild wastewood, beyond the boggy fields and the low mountain, the Irish Sea gleams silver in the sun, or dulls to slate under cloud. For some species, that stretch of water is too dangerous to try to cross; for others, migrants, it is a road. It's far away, that road or barrier, but ever present as the frontier of the country in which I live. Everywhere, near and far, there are permeable boundaries like that, tenuously guarding an inside and an outside – my country, my community, my garden, my house, my bedroom. Everywhere, near at hand and far off, those permeable boundaries seek to keep real or notional threats at bay: threats to limited resources, or solitude, or physical wellbeing, or control or convenience, and above all some real or imagined threat of change.

The threat of change is what the swallows confront

me with more urgently every year: the threat to them, and the much lesser threat to me. Because to let them in to nest, to embrace their mess and noise in my living space, seems to risk challenging something basic in my human identity, which is my essential separation from all other non-domesticated species. And to do that voluntarily would put me outside the boundary of socially sanctioned behaviour; it would risk making me seem unclean.

In the view of some people, that is already the case, because of where I draw the line. One morning when I met an acquaintance after a night disrupted by mice fighting in the attic, she looked at me with horror when I explained my tiredness. 'You have *mice*?' she exclaimed. 'How repulsive!'

'I live in the country,' I said. 'My house is old and a bit porous.'

'Can't you block up the holes?' she said, shuddering.

I wondered how to explain just how porous an old stone cottage could be, but I could see that I would only make it worse. Another acquaintance told me once: 'I like to look at nature – from the car. I don't really want contact with it. How can you bear to live in the country?' But the deep horror of a friend towards the natural world – a full-blown phobia about other living things, even house plants – was far less alien. His phobia, in which he experienced everything alive as potentially contaminating, made a certain kind of sense to me. Perhaps his horror at proximity to other living species is similar to how I feel about urban life, with its close proximity to crowds of people: claustrophobic, panicky, and under threat. Even the idea of living in close proximity to one other human is challenging, because of the loss of autonomy and loss of self that it would entail. My need for solitude might not extend to other species, but when it comes to fellow humans I am much more inclined to impose controls on my environment.

The mice or voles are welcome to use my walls, my attic; I don't mind the sound of them above me, unless they keep me awake fighting, or scurrying back and forth building up stores. In a good hazelnut year, that can be a long and noisy process. One autumn, a mouse must have transported an entire winter's supply into the attic, and it must have been a small mouse, a wood mouse, perhaps, because it struggled to carry its find, and kept dropping nuts on the attic floor with a sharp percussion above my head. Some of them it lost: I found a hazelnut on my bedroom floor and another in the laundry basket. One time, after I'd left a bowl of chestnuts by the woodburner, I found chestnuts stored in my boots.

Maybe accepting the presence of non-human species in my house places me beyond the bounds of familiar human behaviour, but I draw the line at sharing my immediate living space with anyone. I limit woodworm, though I can't eradicate it. If newts or slugs or stray sheep come in, I put them out. The mice and voles are safe from me in the attic, but if they start using my bedroom or kitchen or living room, I set traps, because they chew everything. They do it in a random, experimental way that makes it impossible to repair damage, taking chunks out of fabric, plastic, paper; destroying boxes, sheets, a duvet. Even when they find the material is inedible they have another go a little further on, or on the other side, as if to test if that's still true. I could use a live trap, and then transport them a couple of miles away and release them, but it seems cruel to terrify a vole in this way, and then terrify it again by releasing it in unfamiliar territory. Trapping and releasing them also displaces responsibility for causing their death, even if the killer is then a buzzard or an owl rather than a trap. So I kill them myself, and then put the delicate little furry corpses out in the wood for someone else to have as food.

Tolerating rodents in your house, even if they aren't crapping in your food, probably falls on the wrong side of the socially accepted line of cleanliness for most people. If I were to be assessed, say, as a foster parent, or wanted to adopt, I doubt I would pass: officially, I might be classed as living in squalor. Still, I watch a blackbird preening, or sunning itself, wings and tail spread, and think how strange it is that being dirty, and living in squalor, should be associated with 'living like an animal'. A blackbird might spend a third of its day looking after its feathers, cleaning and oiling them, zipping together all the tiny barbules, keeping them in good repair. Most birds and mammals are fastidious about staying clean for reasons of survival: feathers and fur in good order keeps parasites under control and maintains a working barrier against the cold and the wet, and against vulnerability to disease. They are not, by any measure, unclean.

But our fear of contamination has more to do with what might be in their gut, in their droppings, in among their feathers or fur, than to do with the living creature itself. On mites, ticks, fleas, amoebas, I am in agreement with most people: the idea of having these species in my living space, or on (or in) my person, is anathema, and I would take extreme measures against any such uninvited visitors. Perhaps if I were to look up images of the intestinal parasites that voles carry, I might act differently, but in this, for now, I choose ignorance.

While I might differ from some on the proximity of voles and mice, on rats I draw the line in a more conventional place. In part it's because of the deep historical and cultural association with disease and dirt and rubbish; in part it's because of their ability to get in, despite the measures you take, and to cause ruin and leave filth. Unlike other rodents, the brown rat threatens as a species that you can't control. Their reminder that no barrier is impenetrable makes them a powerfully effective image of risk, real or imagined, so that depicting people as rats or in the company of rats resonates with some of our most deeply held notions of threat, and loathing, and the fearful need for control or eradication.

I don't loathe rats, but I understand the fear and hatred that those depictions are intended to evoke, because I feel this about wasps. Not all wasps, though: not large, delicate wood wasps, or the little turquoise and red parasitic wasps – just the vile yellow-and-black-striped paper wasp with its nightmare weaving aggression and loathsome articulated body and vindictive face.

My response to wasps is visceral and compulsive. It is a state of deep loathing. I don't want so much to avoid or destroy wasps, as for wasps not to exist. I want them utterly eradicated, to never have existed: their very existence is contaminating and repulsive.

I will talk to the bee that accidentally wanders into my house and fetches up against the window, but not the wasp that invades my home and writhes at the glass. I'll place a cup over a bee, slide a piece of paper under to lift it off the window and then carry it outside and release it. But for a wasp I'll fetch a book – a large, heavy book is best – and press it against the glass until I hear the wasp's hard body crunch and squelch. Even watching its death throes fills me with hatred.

I am not proud of my loathing, or how I deal with it; it is entirely at odds with my approach to the rest of the wild things I live with. But this isn't simple fear of a wasp's stinging threat: it's a phobic loathing. And though I know I should try to address it, even to contemplate doing so feels existentially dangerous, as though I would be letting the barriers down, and allowing a great threat to have agency, and legitimacy.

If ever I wanted to live in a sealed box and believe in impenetrable barriers, it is in the summer months, when wasps emerge in teeming, threatening striped hoards, pinging at me if I'm outside, sending me scurrying indoors. I'm not sure I can change my response to them, because at some deep level I don't *want* to change how I feel. I loathe wasps, and part of loathing is wanting to loathe. Loathing entails not making room for anything that might make your loathing weaken: it relies on seeing the object of your loathing as vile and without value.

When the next queen wasp emerges, I'll hear her first, before I see her – quietly rasping at the rough fence, peeling off tiny wood fibres. She'll fly off with her bright yellow mandibles full of shavings, and will stop frequently at the pond for water. Slowly over days she will build the fragile, complex paper cells of her nest, like a great balloon of crisp-baked beaten egg white. Grudgingly, trying to control my revulsion at what it will house, I can imagine her making her nest. Could I let her do that – in the attic, or under the eaves, or adjacent to the apartment complex of the solitary bees above my door? Could I leave her be, knowing what it would lead to: hundreds, thousands of wasps later in the year? Probably not, because loathing is not easily undone. But perhaps I could start with one wasp that wanders in. Perhaps I could control my fear, and afford it the same consideration, the same treatment that I afford a bee. The fact that I loathe it and fear it and want it not to exist, want its entire species not to exist, does not justify placing a different value on it from the mason bee or honey bee that enters my house. Perhaps starting with one wasp could begin the undoing of my loathing, wasp by wasp, and the undoing of my desire to loathe.

When I address a bee that has got in and is bumping against the window, it takes on an existence as someone else who is sharing my space. I don't think I am anthropomorphising, projecting any human characteristic or personality onto that bee, or onto the mouse who I tell to shut up with her clamour with the hazelnuts: it feels instead simply like a breaking down of my human isolation from it. As a result, it becomes some*one*, rather than some*thing*.

Conversely, when I see a living thing as an intruder, part of an undifferentiated mass, a representative of a teeming horrorscape, I strip it of its individual autonomy and legitimacy and agency; I make it into a thing. In the same way, explicitly or implicitly to call any group of humans vermin is to strip them of regard, and of rights; it renders them subject to control and eradication. Some of the same process is perhaps in play in the reduction of a woman from an autonomous individual, worthy of equal regard, to something that may be controlled. I know how being reduced to an existence of lesser value can make you believe you are of lesser value, and though I doubt it is in a wasp's experience to value itself one way or another, the experience of having been reduced like this gives me pause.

For me wasps are some*thing*, not someone. Providing a home for this kind of loathing enables me to disregard a whole species, and treat it as disposable, the way as a species we treat whole universes of insects as disposable. Our rivers are emptier as a result, though we hardly notice it. Our skies are emptier too, visibly so: emptier of insects, and emptier of the birds that live on them – flycatchers, house martins, swifts, swallows.

Last year, friends everywhere asked, 'Have you had any swallows? There are so few swallows this spring.' Nest sites that had been used for decades remained unvisited, and other nests failed. Fewer birds had raised young, or had survived their long migration to Africa, and their winter there; others had not survived their long migration back. The reasons seem complicated and various, but one of them is the increasing scarcity of the insects that they eat.

I thought last year, when swallows came skimming through my garden, I would face that old dilemma again – whether to shut the door against them, or let them in. But I had left it too late. Last year, for the first time, no swallow came and investigated the doorway to my home. Up the road from me, two barns and an open garage had been converted. Now there are no swallows in the village at all.

7. Meetings at Dusk

It was June, and warm, and the nightjars had returned. They'd been reported at Cross Inn Forest, where the bit of commercial forestry had been cut a few years ago. In winter, it was home to a lone, much-sought-after northern grey shrike, and I read regular reports of crossbills and occasional goshawks, though when I visited I always failed to see them.

Ideal conditions for hearing a nightjar are warm still evenings, which, in that clear-cut, meant midges. I prepared myself for the encounter, and dressed appropriately. Though it would make me uncomfortably hot, I wore long socks under jeans that covered my ankles, a snood over my hair, and a scarf over that to protect my ears and face and neck. Before I got out of the car I turned on the interior light and applied Smidge liberally. Checking myself in the mirror to make sure I did not miss some bit of exposed skin, I wondered briefly what another person might make of this get-up – whether they'd note the binoculars, and see a birdwatcher armoured against midges, or whether they'd note my brown skin, and see the scarf as a hijab.

I got out of the car, and slipped round the closed gate of the forestry track. I quelled my habitual unease about walking alone at night: there had been no other cars in the lay-by, so I had the place to myself.

The clear-cut had created a unique habitat. Where once there had been a lightless, acid canopy, a monoculture for miles, now there was rotting wood, thick brash, and a new heathland of low birch and hazel and heather. Here and there, the drainage ditches that used to run between the old stands of close-planted conifers were open pools of standing water, and the insect life was vigorous and voracious.

The midges brushed against me as I set off along the track, but they didn't land or bite, not at first, not while the Smidge was still working. It was not so much walking through clouds of midges as walking through a loosely adhering organism: hanging swags of them parted when I moved, but closed up around me when I stopped to listen or to look.

I knew this was almost certainly a doomed outing. It never works when I go looking for something – not the California gray whales passing close in at the Point

Reyes lighthouse, on their migration north to Alaska; not otters on Mull, and not the goshawks here at Cross Inn Forest. No species ever appears or performs for me if I go looking, so I was trying not to search or strain to hear. I wanted to hear nightjars that were being nightjars for one another, not for a recording. I was hoping for an authentic experience of nightjars, a natural experience, not one that had been curated. Somehow, I felt I could not yet say I'd heard a nightjar, definitively, until I'd heard it without another's intervention.

The sun had set, but it was not yet dark, and I'd only walked a few hundred metres when I heard voices ahead of me – a loud child, adults, a dog yapping. I was glad it was not a lone man, even one with binoculars, but I was disappointed to have my expectations confirmed: even if the nightjars had been there, they'd have probably gone elsewhere now, with those voices.

Round the bend came the human inconvenience: a boy running ahead, about eight or nine, whacking with a stick at the willowherb beside the path. When he spotted me, he stopped, looked round at his parents, and hurried back to them. They glanced at me, and then they looked at one another, and then they didn't look at me again. The Jack Russell behind them hadn't yet noticed me, and the woman stopped and picked it up, and then it began to growl. As I drew near, I wished them 'Noswaith dda', but they didn't answer. The boy stared at me, but his parents looked rigidly past me into the darkening distance ahead of them. The dog's steady growl increased as I approached, and it turned its head and watched me walking past, growling all the while. I heard their footsteps moving away behind me, and when they reached the next bend, one of them began to talk again, but I couldn't make out what they were saying, and then they were round the curve and there was no longer any sign of them. But they'd left behind them their crackling hostility, unspoken but tangible, and with it the wound of loneliness when you are placed outside a human bond.

All my thought of nightjars was gone; all thought of birds, all awareness of the evening chorus around me had been erased by their hostility. It could have been any number of things, I told myself; it was not necessarily what I thought it was. *Don't jump to conclusions*, my little inner voice said – *you can't know*, though I thought I did know.

I wish I was never self-conscious like that, never had to second-guess myself, never had to try to convince myself, as I tried to do then, that I was imagining something. I wish it were possible to walk somewhere rural or wild, and not be braced against the ever-present possibility of hostility. But it doesn't go away, early experience – and my early experience taught me that to be brown in a rural place is to be asked implicitly or explicitly what you're doing there, to give an account of where you're from, to be told you don't belong. In Britain, if you're brown in a rural place, you're always seen as being from somewhere else.

As a young child, I was hardly aware that other children didn't look like me. *You're lucky*, girls said to me in the changing rooms, *you've got brown legs even in winter*, but it was the beginning of adolescence when I became self-conscious about looking different from those around me. At first it was just the trade of any available hurtful insult – *Paki, nig-nog*; later, shouts from parked cars (*go home jungle-bunny*), or sotto voce but carefully within my hearing, and more ethnically accurate (and rather rhythmically compelling): *once a Jew, always a Jew, and the only good Jew is a dead Jew*. Early on, parka-wearing Kevin, with whom I and two friends were smoking an illicit first cigarette, gave me his version of *The Protocols of the Elders of Zion* as it pertained to my people in general, and my father and me in particular. Later, as I got older, it was the ever-recurring tedious question, 'Where are you from?' (answer: 'Sussex'), and its follow-on, 'I mean where are you from *originally*?' It may not be meant as hostility but its effect is always one of exclusion.

I no longer try to answer that question; I try to head it off, and its follow-on, by stating where I live. The answer, that I live near Tregaron, didn't satisfy a man in a bar in Shrewsbury, once I'd explained that Tregaron was near Aberystwyth. 'You don't look like you're from Aberystwyth,' he said, smiling. 'Why, what do people from Aberystwyth look like?' I asked, not returning his smile. 'Whiter,' he said, and laughed, as though to communicate to me how well he understood the blighted whiteness of rural Wales that I must experience.

'Oh, you're such a lovely colour,' said a woman serving me coffee in a campus café at Swansea University. 'Where are you from?' The deflection rarely works, and it didn't that time either. 'I live in Ceredigion,' I said. 'No, but where's your *family* from?' she asked. 'You're something dark, aren't you?'

It's not something I ever encountered when I lived in California. In the multi-ethnic Bay Area it was my accent, not my appearance, that provoked the question – and there were never the follow-up questions about origins: instead I was for the first time unquestionably, unambiguously English. Immigration, in the US, means something quite different. But so too does race.

I was dismayed, but not surprised, when I read

what happened to Chris Cooper, the birdwatcher in New York's Central Park who had the police called on him by an angry dogwalker a few hours before George Floyd was killed in 2020. It could have been a benign encounter between a dogwalker letting her dog run free and someone pointing out that dogs must be on a lead in that protected area of the park. But instead she refused to leash her dog, and told him: 'I'm going to call the cops and tell them an African American man is threatening my life.' He filmed her calling 911 and saying to the dispatcher in a breathless, agitated voice: 'There's an African American man; I'm in Central Park; he's recording me, and threatening myself and my dog.' Fortunately, by the time the police arrived, they'd both left.

If, walking alone somewhere, I were to see a woman with binoculars coming towards me, I don't know if I'd see her as a birdwatcher first and a woman second. But if a man with binoculars came towards me, I suspect he would always be a man first, and a birdwatcher second. I don't know what different socially learned reactions would kick in if he were a person of colour, because whether I'm in rural Wales, England or Scotland, the people I see with binoculars (usually men) are always, without exception, white.

'I don't know whether she's a racist or not,' Chris

Cooper said in an interview after the incident was widely shared on social media and in the press. 'I don't know her life, I don't know how she lives it. That *act* was unmistakeably racist, even if she didn't realise it in the moment.' The confrontation, and the widespread media coverage it triggered, revealed a particular expression of America's deep racism. It highlighted who may and who may not have access to the natural world without barriers imposed by other people. In the wake of Cooper's experience, the Twitter campaign, #BlackBirdersWeek, which was launched by a group of Black researchers and students working in natural science, gave a high profile to people of colour in Britain too, and illustrated prejudices and assumptions about who works in the natural sciences and in the countryside, and who is and is not entitled to an unquestioned enjoyment of rural space.

America's version of the countryside, and the legacy of control and exclusivity of rural space – particularly in the Confederate states – is so different from Britain's that there is hardly a point of comparison to be made. The overt racial shaping of wilderness in the US – either entirely emptying it of indigenous people both physically and by an act of imagination, or romanticising those lives into idealised 'living in harmony' Stone Age absurdity – is in a rough and general way widely acknowledged. In contrast, the very different racial shaping of the rural and wild places of Britain has hardly been recognised at all.

But there have been changes; there is the beginning of a public conversation about the way in which the imagined idyll of the British countryside, along with its romanticised wild hinterland, has been established and perpetuated as white space. Part of that conversation took place in the wake of the Black Lives Matter movement, and the incident in New York City. But quite a vigorous debate had already occurred two years earlier, after the results of a popular poll on the UK's 'favourite' work of nature writing were made public. Initiated by the Landlines nature writing research project at Leeds University and promoted by the BBC, the poll had asked the public to vote on a shortlist of nature writing books, and the results were published in early 2018. Second place went to *Tarka the Otter*, a dark and tragic tale of otter hunting and otter survival that haunted my childhood in which there were no longer any otters. The book, published in 1927, is celebrated for turning public opinion in favour of otters, and transforming them from hated vermin into one of Britain's best-loved mammals. But as bird writer Richard Smyth pointed out in an article in the *New Humanist*, the author, Henry Williamson, was a fervent Nazi. According to Smyth, although Williamson's political views are known, they have been elided (in that popular poll, at least) in part because of unexamined assumptions about the 'natural' relationship between conservation concerns and politically progressive attitudes. '*Tarka* gets a free pass,' he remarked. 'The rectitude of nature writing is taken as read.'

Perhaps that free pass, that sense of nature writing being above such tainting associations, belongs now to the lost state of purported innocence that predated the death of George Floyd and the threat to birdwatcher Chris Cooper in Central Park – that comfortable Eden before #BlackBirdersWeek and #BlackAFinSTEM spotlit how the right of entry into rural and wild places is not the same for everyone. Perhaps now in the UK it will no longer be possible to gloss over the question of racism in the nature writing of the past and the silence about it, nor to ignore the experience (and expertise) of people of colour in the natural world.

But resistance is strong, particularly where there are powerful attachments to classics of children's literature whose otherworldly magic, as adults, we are so reluctant to relinquish. The reluctance, where

Tarka the Otter is concerned, is understandable, if not defensible (there is similarly strong resistance to adjusting the celebratory embrace of Roald Dahl, despite his clearly articulated and well-documented antisemitism). *Tarka* is about otters, so perhaps it's easy to make a separation between the author's attitudes and some of his work. Certainly, the Henry Williamson Society appears able to compartmentalise. A note on its website states rather modestly, 'Henry Williamson has been much criticised for his involvement with fascism,' and includes a link to a formal 'Statement on Fascism' which reads: 'The Henry Williamson Society does not support nor promote Fascism in any way whatever and entirely dissociates itself from any organisations which have misrepresented it as doing so. From its inception the Society has sought to further the appreciation of Henry Williamson's literary work. It is non-political and is dedicated to its literary aim: to encourage interest in and a deeper understanding of the life and work of Henry Williamson.'

Smyth didn't give *Tarka* a free pass, and nor did he offer one to nature writing more generally. 'The landscape of modern writing on nature is haunted by the ghosts of fascism,' he observed. 'Williamson was a Nazi – a ruralist, a naturalist, naïve and solitary, but a Nazi too, a fervent admirer of "the great man across the Rhine" and an adherent of Oswald Mosley's British Union of Fascists.' Smyth's exploration of 'The Dark Side of Nature Writing' in 2018 made sobering reading, and provoked a great deal of discussion, not least about the equally troubling risk he identifies in the ecology and conservation movement, where racism and green politics find themselves such easy bedfellows. 'There are live themes in the green debate – beyond simple-minded volkish notions of the white English yeoman,' he states, 'to which reactionary ideas can be readily attached.'

Those volkish notions of the white English yeoman are powerful and pervasive far beyond environmental writing and discussion, and I, for one, internalised them. It is precisely such volkish notions that determined my early experience of living in a rural place: the notion of a rooted peasantry; ancient stock; deep tradition; folkloric survival of history and community, and above all, belonging to the land, a land whose people, shaping it for millennia, invest it with particular local meaning. As a child, it was evident around me in the families who'd farmed in Sussex for generations; it was there in the disappearing rural Sussex accent and in the place names of Ashdown Forest. Volkish notions of the relationship between people, mythology and land pervaded the teaching in the Steiner school that I attended, and the philosophy behind it (something that continues to be a matter of contention in the world of Steiner education). But more insidiously, it was implicit (and sometimes explicit) in the children's literature I read: Susan Cooper's *The Dark Is Rising* sequence; *Moon Stallion*; Arthur Ransome's *Swallows and Amazons* books (particularly *The Coot Club*, set in the Norfolk Broads); Enid Blyton's nice white boys and girls and swarthy bad men; Malcolm Saville's Shropshire birdwatching children; JRR Tolkien's *The Hobbit* and *The Lord of the Rings*; Alan Garner's books set around Alderley Edge, and TH White's *The Once and Future King*.

Many of those works in one way or another engage with an idea of local folklore, tradition or legend representing the continued existence of deeper forces held in the land (at the Neolithic site of Waylands Smithy, for example) and, importantly, in the people of that land. Or they deal with the power of ancient paths, of chalk figures such as the White Horse at Uffington. So much of the children's literature that I read invested these rural places with numinous, mythical power, a sense of an ancient past still present in the landscape, and they privileged the connection between that land and the people whose families had deep roots in it. As was the case for many children of the 1970s – and some of the most noted current crop of English nature writers – the books that were formative for my sense of place, and in particular of mid Wales, were the five volumes of Susan Cooper's *The Dark Is Rising*, in which heroic characters like Will or Old George carry ethnic memory, blood memory. They are people from ancient stock: they are *indigenous*.

Of course you can't opt into what's indigenous. You might identify with it, but you can't claim it as yours if you're not from there. There is a shadow root of *beget* in the word indigenous, as though the land itself begets you. Indigenous, native: both mean 'natural' etymologically and semantically, but though natural, like native, may have its roots in *nasci*, to be born, being born in a place isn't sufficient to make you indigenous; it cannot make you innate.

Immigrants can only be indigenous to the place they emigrated from; the second and subsequent generations aren't indigenous to anywhere. Without family roots in the place you're born, you always carry the taint of being an introduced species. You might adopt a cultural tradition, a particular relationship to a specific place, a specific land, but they're not *really* ever yours, not authentically.

That is how you're seen, even if it's not how you feel. And others' perceptions about your family's origins shape how you feel about where you are, even if your family's origins did not do so in the first place. *Where are you from*, they ask. *No, but where's your family from – where are you from originally?* Because if you're brown in rural England, in rural Wales, you're always from elsewhere.

Indigenous is a neutral descriptor only if it refers to an oppressed minority; it's hostile and exclusive if it refers to an oppressive majority. 'The indigenous British', 'the indigenous English', 'the indigenous Welsh', 'the indigenous language of the British Isles' – if I hear or read those terms, I wince. With the exception of citing Welsh as an indigenous language in order to challenge the 'speak English' xenophobia directed at migrants, I know what identity group and accompanying set of attitudes is usually being evoked, consciously or otherwise: white, anti-immigrant, nativist, ruralist, fascist.

The distinction between some notional indigenous population and those who are not 'from' here operates implicitly in rural places throughout the UK, no matter how many people of colour are included in broadcast dramas set in Pembrokeshire or Cumbria, in Ceredigion or the fictional public service announcement county of *The Archers*. If you're brown in Ambridge or Aberystwyth, the presumption is that you're *from* somewhere else (*Where are you from? No, where are you from originally, I mean where are your parents from?*) and this, therefore, becomes your own internalised reality too. Which is part of why, if you're brown in a white space, you are always checking for signs, preparing for the challenge, steeling yourself against the reaction that suggests you don't belong, that states implicitly, and often explicitly, that you are not a part of, but apart from. And it's partly why, in the absence of interfering human meanings in a wild place, the whole question of belonging or not belonging, being part of or apart from, can fade for a while into nothingness.

What did this couple at Cross Inn Forest mean, with their cold, looking-away silence? Perhaps they had been in the middle of an argument; perhaps they were socially awkward; perhaps they never spoke to anyone they met while out walking their dog. I couldn't know. All I could know was how it affected me. In rather typically British style, nothing had been said, but nevertheless a great deal had been said. Confirmation bias, someone might say – and yes, it's true: early experience readied me for hostility, and subsequent experience reinforced it.

But there are also challenges to my biases. One hot July day, when I went for a run along the narrow road towards Swyddffynnon, I was already primed for a confrontation with a driver. The banks were overgrown, with nettles and heavy seed-heads weighing down the long grass, which narrowed the already narrow road, leaving no room for a car and a pedestrian to safely pass one another. It was a sultry day, humid and overcast. The still air was thick with low-flying insects, and swallows were skimming near the ground and along the softening tarmac. I'd run three miles, and I was sweating heavily, when a car, coming towards me, pulled to the side and stopped. It had an English plate; I assumed it was driven by a tourist. As I drew close, the driver, a heavy, middle-aged balding white man shouted from the open window, 'You ain't right!' in a London accent. Was this just hostility for presuming to use the road and annoyingly slow him down, or was it going to be something worse? 'What do you mean I'm not right?' I asked, slowing as I passed, and then running backwards, registering how, defensively, unconsciously, I had poshed up what he'd asked. Was he going to react to that too? 'Runnin',' he shouted. *Runnin'* – and he shook his head with pity, making a wide gesture that took in the heat, the hill he'd just come down, the whole hot hostile world outside his safe cool car.

*

In the darkening forestry, the Smidge was starting to lose its strength, or the insects were worse: they weren't landing, but they were making contact. I got as far as the open land where the track reaches a T-junction, and then turned back, ill at ease. There were no nightjars. A late and annoyingly loud song thrush on a high branch at the edge of the uncut trees was repeating and repeating, blocking out quieter sounds. There were smaller, unidentifiable calls, the repeated quiet *tzeep-tzeep* of young birds, a snatch of robin song. Then on the heathland a grasshopper warbler started up and that was almost as good as what I'd hoped to hear. If it had not been for that human encounter I might not have walked that far, and might not have heard the warbler.

But on my way back, the nightjars began.

Unheimlich, I thought, afterwards – reaching for a word that has no strict equivalent in English: eerie, uncanny, but really meaning the familiar made other. Everything about *heimlich* undone, in both of its original meanings: homely, comfortable, known, but also hidden, secret, private. So that in Freud's exploration of the word and of the literary depiction of the uncanny, *unheimlich* is the undoing of both those meanings: the familiar made other, and what should be hidden (from consciousness, at least) revealed. That's what the nightjar did to me: it revealed something about the hidden space that is the wild world at twilight, that strange transitional time when mystical transformations occur in folklore and myth. But at midsummer, when it never gets fully dark, twilight is not a transition but a state, and the nightjar's eerie continuous churring, a multi-directional, unlocateable sound, was its aural expression.

I wondered whether that was what the couple had experienced when they'd seen me – perhaps I had made their world unheimlich, in the way that their response made the world unheimlich for me. Perhaps that's what an encounter with the Other always does. It makes the familiar world unfamiliar, and reveals what is usually hidden: the tenuousness of your feeling at home in the world.

The churring of the nightjar continued without stopping. The same word, to churr, might be used for grasshoppers, and cicadas, but this long, low, continuous vibrating sound was nothing like a cicada or a grasshopper. It changed pitch occasionally, and in the distance another began, and then a third. I glimpsed one in flight, low over the clear-cut, and tried to find it through my binoculars, but as I changed the focus, there was a strange, frightening clacking sound. Someone was near me. I looked around but couldn't see anyone. I pushed my scarf and snood away from my ears, risking getting bitten, and then the sound came again, close by, very close, sharp like an irregular repeated blow. In the dusk I saw the nightjar, hovering three feet from me above the path, and I realised, relieved, that I was hearing for the first time the other sound that nightjars make: it was clapping its wings in a mating display.

There is no other bird I have seen that has made me feel so full of delight and so ill at ease. Perhaps it was the oddness of only glimpsing them in the deepening dusk, their strange shape and floppy flight; perhaps it was the association in their other name, *goatsucker*, and that tradition, from Aristotle via Pliny, that they secretly suckle goats dry – a piece of folklore that links them, irretrievably, if only by association, to incubi, succubi and vampires. Or perhaps it was my unease about other humans that predisposed me to feel ill at ease with any encounter with the Other. But birdwatchers I've spoken to who've seen and heard nightjars report the same feeling: nightjars are eerie, uncanny, in a way that no other bird is, so that it's easy to understand the fearful rural folklore associated with them.

And then my unease sharpened: I heard footsteps approaching along the path. There was a man coming towards me with a large Alsatian, and suddenly I was aware – acutely, sharply aware – of being a woman alone in the dark.

It isn't usually fear, exactly, my reaction: I just feel profoundly alert, adrenaline readying me to respond to a possible threat. But when the man saw me, he guided his panting, eager dog to his offside, moved over to the edge of the path to give me a wide berth, greeted me warmly, smiling as he passed, and without slowing, he strode away down the track.

Who knows what he meant by his action, and who knows what that couple meant. Perhaps it doesn't matter, because it's what you do that has weight; it's what you do, not what you mean, that has consequences. This man saw me, appeared to recognise the potential feeling of threat to me, a woman alone at night, and with his body and his voice he reassured me – perhaps unconsciously, perhaps deliberately. In an instant, he restored all the warmth and familiarity of human social bonds, restored my sense of *heimlichkeit*, and made me feel for a moment at home in the world.

8. What's in a Name?

I was shocked when I saw it – a photograph of American birdwatchers that was straight out of *Ocean's Eleven*: five fit and attractive men, laden with tech, in cool outdoor gear walking down an empty road. 'One year ago I starred in that birding heist movie,' tweeted birder Nate Swick, when he posted the photo, taken for a US magazine in 2019. Twitter users quickly photoshopped in background explosions, and added movie soundtracks. You could feel the hidden mayhem they'd left behind, somewhere out of sight in the background – the birds hunted down and ticked; the stand-off about identification of subspecies; the boastful tales over shot glasses of rotgut; the accounts of MEGAs and RAREs, and of the injuries sustained getting to them. In place of handguns and stun grenades they carried binoculars (light, small, compact), and instead of sniper rifles, they wielded telescopes and cameras.

These men were birdwatchers, and they were *cool*. They were even – dare I think it, let alone say it? – *sexy*.

One of them – Nick Lund, aka @TheBirdist – was also funny. I'd originally discovered him on Twitter when he'd asked for help identifying the birdsong in the opening rainforest sequence of *Raiders of the Lost Ark* (it was a recording of a British dawn chorus with added howler monkeys). He took birdwatching knowledge to interesting places – for example scrutinising Google Street View footage for the background birds its cameras captured – and periodically, with very dry humour, he'd give an illustrated account of the latest battle to outwit chipmunk raiders of his bird-feeders.

A hundred and fifty years earlier, all that gear would have been guns, and their clothes would have been breeches and canvas gaiters. They'd have been on horseback, at ease in the saddle, or on board ship, boldly going where no white man had gone before, and where no one but a naturalist would choose to go, either: into the deserts and thickets and malarial marshes of existing or future European colonies, shooting and laying claim in acts of imperial pillage and profit for which they continue to be honoured in the names they imposed on every bird species they identified as 'new' – which is to say new to Western knowledge.

The basement archives of the Liverpool World Museum are cool and dim. It's a sultry day in July, humid and thundery, and the air-conditioning is not working in the hotel where I'm staying, so it's a relief to sit here in the cool air, waiting for my first sight of the birds shot in Palestine by the English naturalist Henry Baker Tristram. The collection that he sold to the Liverpool Museum in 1896 numbered more than 20,000 skins, and although some were lost during the Second World War, most of that early collection was preserved. Others, including the more than 24,000 eggs he collected, ended up in the Natural History Museum at Tring and elsewhere in the UK and the US.

It's hard to imagine the sheer volume of birds that used to fill the sky and land in the nineteenth century, when Tristram was compiling his collections, just as, perhaps, it will be hard for a child growing up now to imagine the volume of insects that used to fly, in our living memory, over a hay meadow or above a river. Tristram was known as the Great Gun of Durham, a nickname that surely contributed to him being described as one of the 'great sportsmen and bird slaughterers of the late nineteenth and early twentieth century', but, as Tristram's biographer points out, 'The Great Gun of Durham' was a punning nickname conferred by a friend, on the occasion of Tristram being made canon of Durham Cathedral.

Nevertheless, although Tristram was not indiscriminate in his shooting of birds, the acquisition by the Liverpool Museum of this collection of more than 20,000 bird-skins indicates the sheer scale of his collecting – some of it through trade and purchase, but the vast majority by his own gun, or by the guns of those whom he paid what he disparagingly called 'backshish'.

The oldest birds in the collection are a male and female Tristram's grackle, now more commonly referred to as Tristram's starling. It is probably the best-known bird that carries Tristram's name, because it is present in noisy abundance at Masada, one of the prime tourist sites in Israel (and a prime birdwatching site during the migration season). The grackle's haunting melodious whistle, a little like the call of a golden oriole, though higher pitched, is distinctive, and its orange wings make it unlike any other bird that it might at first glance resemble (even if an American tourist might think of a red-winged blackbird, in size and shape it is very different).

Shot near the Dead Sea in 1858, the two grackles in the Liverpool collection are mere skin and feathers, beak and feet, the empty eye sockets shrivelled. The female's brown feathers are a little faded, and the glossy black feathers of the male are dull; in both, the distinctive orange wing feathers have turned brown with age. They're about the size of a mistle thrush, but their bodies are light as paper, insubstantial.

Behind me, in the archives, there are drawers and drawers full of other birds he shot – some 17,000 of them, each in a protective cellophane wrapper, each with a tag tied to its leg, giving its name, sex, and the location and date it was shot, written in faded ink in Tristram's hand.

These two grackles are the type specimens for the species, and they each have two little cardboard tags tied to their legs: Tristram's catalogue label, with the place and date that the bird was shot, and a red label with the type specimen publication details.

Tristram submitted them as a 'new' species in 1858, and they were described and named in his honour by Philip Sclater in *The Annals and Magazine of Natural History*: 'A pair of this fine species... was obtained by the Rev HB Tristram in Palestine during the present spring,' he reported, 'and I have called it after its discoverer.... Mr Tristram shot these birds on the 30th of March last, at Mar-Saaba, in the valley of the Hebron. They had their nest in the rocks; but he was unable to reach it.'

I wish there were a record of that 1858 visit that Tristram made to Palestine, but all that remains is an account of the birds he collected, which appeared in the first issue of the journal *Ibis* (he'd co-founded the journal, along with the British Ornithological Union, in 1859, and both the journal and the organisation were, allegedly, conceived of in his drawing room in Durham). Fortunately, his next visit to Palestine was recorded in a vivid, evocative adventure story which was published in 1865. *The Land of Israel: A Journal of Travels in Palestine, Undertaken with Special Reference to Its Physical Character,* went into many editions, as did *The Land of Moab*, his account of trying to make a circuit of the Dead Sea in 1872.

Tristram has fascinated me for years. His descriptions of places and birds that I know and love in Israel/Palestine evoke a living landscape of the nineteenth century that had been entirely transformed by the mid-twentieth century. Not all of that transformation was loss: the tiny iridescent Palestine sunbird, which you might now see in gardens anywhere in Israel and the West Bank, had been almost entirely restricted to the Jordan Valley when Tristram was riding around 'obtaining' bird specimens. Often this was from the back of his favourite horse, a chestnut Arab thoroughbred, which, he wrote, had 'become perfectly trained as a shooting-pony, and, with the docility which characterises his race, would implicitly follow the commands of the voice, and, without flinching, allow me to traverse my gun between his ears.' Tristram was so taken by the sunbird that he enthusiastically shot some two dozen of them in 1863 and 1864, and there are seventeen of their tiny skins in the Liverpool Museum, the feathers of the males still retaining their purple and green iridescence more than 150 years after they were killed.

Of all the new birds he encountered in Palestine, this one delighted Tristram the most. Carefully objective in his description of most birds, he almost always spilled over with enthusiasm when the subject was the sunbird. He referred to it as 'the lovely little sunbird' and 'the gorgeous little sunbird, resplendent in the light' in *The Land of Israel*; as a 'beautiful gem' in *Ibis*, and as 'a tiny little creature of gorgeous plumage, rivalling the hummingbirds of America in the metallic lustre of its feathers, green and purple, with brilliant red and orange plumes under its shoulders', in *The Natural History of the Bible*. Tristram narrowly missed the opportunity to 'discover' the Palestine sunbird.

Annoyingly for him, the privilege of describing and formally naming the species for posterity (and, perhaps, for national glory) had gone to a Frenchman, the ornithologist Charles Bonaparte, who had been sent a specimen in 1856. But though Tristram missed the chance to name the sunbird, he was soon able to claim himself the expert on it, because everywhere that he saw them during his second visit to Palestine, he shot and skinned them – male, female and juveniles. He took their eggs and fledglings, and removed their nests, and described in detail their appearance, behaviour, song, calls, and habitat. For ten days he kept three nestlings alive in a box, and then when he and his companions broke camp to move on, he released the two survivors to their parents.

Tristram's relentless travel and collecting made him the authority on the ornithology of Palestine, and his work has been of lasting value, not least because he was, according to Israeli ornithologist Hadoram Shirihai, so unusually assiduous in his record-keeping. In *The Birds of Israel*, Shirihai describes Tristram's publications as being 'among the most important ornithological sources for comparing changes in the avifauna of Israel'.

But Tristram was not alone in those travels, and while he often acknowledges the work of the other Englishmen who were with him, shooting and skinning, photographing and collecting, his attitude to the many individuals who contributed to his collections and knowledge is largely marked by denigration or omission. That includes the invisible women who fed him and cleaned for him and cared for his children while he was off seeking adventure and recognition – the women who wrote up his notes, catalogued his new acquisitions and dusted his displays (one of Tristram's daughters reported hating the tedium of dusting). And it includes the many men, mostly Bedouin, who cooked and carried, guarded and guided, collected specimens on his behalf, and shared with him a natural history expertise that he never acknowledged.

Most of them remain unidentified, but Tristram does name one: Gemil, a brother of Sheik Mohamed, who was head of the Ghawârineh tribe. Gemil accompanied Tristram on several occasions and in several locations, both in 1864 – when they spent months together in the Jordan valley and travelling down the western side of the Dead Sea – and again in 1872, when Tristram tried to make a full circuit of the Dead Sea.

In *The Land of Israel*, Tristram observed: 'Several of our guards became much interested in our collections, or rather in the backshish which a good specimen calls forth. One of them, Gemil, the brother of our Sheikh, who afterwards became a confidential friend, assisted us greatly, and showed acute powers of discernment.' Confidential, in this sense, meant someone Tristram could rely on, rather than someone in whom he could confide. The page header, 'Native Naturalist', is indicative of the attitude that could never have seen Gemil as an equal, but he could at least accord him a grudging respect. 'Seeing my interest in land shells, he collected them in some quantities, and recognised every species,' Tristram went on. 'This morning with great delight he came and announced he had found a new species in the rocks. I cast a cursory glance at his handful, and told him I had the shell already; upon which he replied I was mistaken, and pointed out a minute but constant difference in the form of the lip between this Helix and the other for which I had taken it, and in which I at once saw he was perfectly correct.' With a little training, he concluded, Gemil 'would soon have made a first-rate collector'.

Gemil served as Tristram's bodyguard wherever they went, except into the water to see if they could wade around a headland, where, 'with true national dislike of the element', he followed Tristram no further.

Tristram's view of those upon whom he depended for safety, access and expertise was ambivalent at best, deeply racist at worst: he saw the Bedouin and fellaheen alike as savages in the most bald imperial understanding of the term. Of one sheikh, he observed: 'Old Abou Dahûk, though the hero of a hundred Arab fights, has nothing of the savage about him, but has a very mild expression of countenance. Like all his followers, he is very dark — not so black as the commonalty, but of a deep olive brown. This may partly arise from the habit of these people, who never wash.'

He depended upon Gemil for his life, and on one occasion at least, Gemil's ingenuity saved him from robbery, and probably from murder. Tristram had separated from those he was travelling with, to spend a few days comparing the fauna and flora near Jericho in spring with what he had already observed in winter. 'I had neither outfit nor servant,' he reported, 'so, having left my money and valuables in the care of my friends, I purchased a tin pot, coffee-pot, plate and cup, laid in a store of biscuit and cheese, ham, coffee, sugar, and figs, and set off, with my muleteer Khadour, and boy Elias, accompanied by my old friend Jemeel of the Ghawârineh' (Tristram might have been a meticulous record-keeper of the natural world, but he was inattentive when it came to Gemil's name: he spelled it variously Gemil, Jemeel and Jemil). On the first night, while he worked on preserving the specimens he'd gathered that day, he was disturbed by the sound of people and animals approaching. Four men from another tribe – with thirteen stolen camels they intended to sell in Jerusalem – stopped at the campsite, and though they were 'armed to the teeth', the only protection Tristram had was his fowling-piece and revolver. It was Gemil who saved him, bringing Tristram's gun to him by the fire to be loaded four times, going away and secretly unloading it each time, a ruse of having numerous weapons that the camel-thieves fell for. Tristram went to bed at last, committing himself 'to God's good keeping in that lonely wilderness'. Despite the protection Gemil had offered him, he did not, apparently, count as company, for Tristram concluded: 'I have often been further from civilisation, but generally with a companion. Here there was a painful intensity in the solitude, enhanced by the beauty of the spot and my strange neighbours.'

In addition to close observation of fine distinctions in types of shell, Gemil was evidently knowledgeable about birds. 'The barer portions of the plain were now occupied by small bands of the

Houbara Bustard,' Tristram wrote, 'whose eggs I sought in vain, though Jemeel, who knew them well, described them admirably.' Eight years later, when he returned, he met up with Gemil again. 'Perhaps his affection was somewhat stimulated by the hope of a new commission,' Tristram observed, 'as he straightway applied for ammunition. We at once equipped him with powder and shot, arsenical soup, and carbolic acid, and bid him meet us in five days, by Jordan. Jemeel certainly did not fail us, and his supply of specimens, when we reached the Jordan plain, attested his industry and prowess, though – alas for my collections! – not his skill in taxidermy.' Evidently Tristram subsequently taught him some rudimentary taxidermy, because later, when they met again, and Gemil presented him with new specimens, including a wildcat, he observed: 'all hinted, by their perfume, that they must be either stowed away or thrown away without delay. Jemeel had, however, profited by his lessons, and had removed the carcasses of the larger beasts.' Among those new specimens for Tristram's collection there were grackles, hoopoes, spotted cuckoos, hawks, and 'desert partridges by the dozen'.

Given this industry, of a kind that Tristram valued and admired, it's jarring to read repeatedly that such interest was only stimulated by the lure of bakshish, a term that Tristram used interchangeably with blackmail, and always with distaste. Perhaps he meant blackmail in its older sense, originating in the payment for protection and patronage that was levied by clans in the so-called Debatable Lands straddling the border between Scotland and Cumbria, but he never saw bakshish as payment of wages, or a fair exchange for labour, but always as some form of bribe. Although he often described individuals and social exchanges with more anthropological objectivity, his work is peppered with views about the inhabitants of Palestine living in filth and squalor, the contemptible manners of the 'natives', who are often described as half-naked savages or bloodthirsty warmongers, all of them greedily eager for bakshish. Poverty, insofar as he recognised it, he attributed to 'Oriental indolence', a term, or variants of it, that recurs repeatedly through several of his books. Observing certain purported ruins of water cisterns, he remarked: 'Did the Bedouin but possess the forethought to preserve or adopt these ancient appliances, they might have water everywhere round these shores; but, like true savages, with the sight and instinct of the keenest red Indian, they are very babes in prevision or prudence.' And, like all peoples whose way of life was intolerable to his Anglican imperial values, the whole of Palestine must be saved by Europe:

'Very rapidly the Bedouin are encroaching wherever horse can be ridden; and the Government is utterly powerless to resist them or to defend its subjects.... Either a European protectorate or union with Egypt seems requisite to save Palestine from gradual dissolution; unless, which seems hopeless, the Arabs can be induced to cultivate the sod.'

Gemil, and many others like him, may not have received recognition for their contribution to scientific understanding in general, and in this case to ornithology in particular, but perhaps in a small way some of that omission is beginning to be acknowledged.

The *Daily Mail* isn't happy about this. 'Now wokeism is coming for the birds!' it exclaimed in 2020, fulminating against a challenge to the names of birds that memorialise troubling historical figures, particularly those guilty of slavery, colonialism, and racist views. In the US, that challenge led to a change in name for McCown's longspur, which had memorialised a confederate general. But in the UK, the response to the campaign was relatively muted, and the *Daily Mail* outrage rather sputtered out in the body of the article, as it reported that the RSPB had invited Flock Together, an inclusive London birdwatchers' group, to take over its Instagram account and discuss problematic names. The Flock Together group suggested that more should be known about the imperial history and exploits behind such names, and they illustrated a handful in their posts – examples of men who had contributed to the expansion of the British Empire. Unlike Bird Names for Birds, one of the American groups that organised the campaign to change the name of the longspur, they did not advocate changing the names.

I wonder what the *Daily Mail* readership, its outrage duly stoked, might make of the approach taken by ornithologists who weighed in for the science community, with substantial arguments about naming conventions. One opinion piece, co-authored by researchers in the UK and the US, provided an overview of previous cases of common bird names being changed. Their cautious, evidence-based arguments in favour of new systems for reconsidering names is hard to argue with: 'Across the world, many of these names were coined from eighteenth- and nineteenth- century European perspectives and are symbolic of a time when this was the only worldview considered in science,' they pointed out. Their case, that 'problematic common names must change if we wish to create a more diverse and inclusive discipline,' is rooted in an argument about the consequences of underrepresentation: 'Promoting diversity and inclusion gives voices to different perspectives that are required for diverse solutions to research questions,' they conclude.

The imperial exploits detailed in Barbara and Richard Mearns' celebratory *Biographies for Birdwatchers* rather underscores that argument, and the book helps illustrate – if inadvertently – why wokism is indeed coming for the birds. Back in 1988, when their compendium was published, the authors were focused on recognition, not reappraisal, and their biographies of the eighty-eight men and three women honoured in the names of birds that are to be found in Europe, Russia, Africa, and the Arctic are lively, colourful, and admiring. The work includes an informative overview of the history of taxonomy and the development of Latin and common naming systems, but it does not touch on the question of who gets to decide who deserves honour for posterity, and for what. Nor does it acknowledge the problem of collecting and exploring as part of advancing the interests of expansionist colonising states as much as the interests of science, or the nefarious impact of such activities, and the structures and racial assumptions underlying them. Many of the sketches read like vivid adventure stories of explorers, and the use of the word 'natives' joltingly evokes a view of empire and 'exploration' that even in 1988 was becoming indefensible.

In their introduction, the authors make a plea for retaining honorifics, arguing that 'the contributions made to the development of ornithology by such men as Charles Bonaparte, George Montagu, Henry Baker Tristram, Georg Stellar and Alexander Wilson deserve to be commemorated by every generation.'

Of those five naturalists, Tristram is perhaps the most obvious British example of the problems that honorific bird names represent, although you have to delve into his out-of-print books to discover the imperial and racist attitudes that make continuing to honour him so troubling.

One solution to the problem of honorific names has been to rename birds after their features – hence 'thick-billed' in place of 'McCown's' in the new name for that American longspur. This seems workable if the feature that you name the bird after is common to both sexes – 'orange-winged starling' in place of 'Tristram's starling' would do fine. But what about sexually dimorphic birds that don't share obvious features like those orange wings? Often, with names based on distinctive features, those features belong to the male alone (the golden oriole could just as well be named the green oriole, for example, while some half of the population of ruffs are always ruff-less).

What if all those birds saddled with a troubling man's name were to be renamed according to the species' female features? Of course it wouldn't be very convenient. In fact it would likely be cumbersome, weighed down with all sorts of strings of adjectives. Tristram's warbler, for example, a North African species, is similar in appearance to two or three others. 'Differs from Spectacled Warbler in its dark throat,' says *Collins* (1972), 'from Subalpine Warbler in lack of white moustache.' Those are descriptions of the male. Of the female it states only: 'female paler.' Paler than what? The female of Tristram's is paler than the male? Paler than the female of the other two? Whichever is meant, the female here is an afterthought. In the accompanying illustrations, the females, positioned in the foreground, but below their respective males, appear strikingly similar to one another, but also subtly distinct. You'd have to pay close attention to those very subtle clues (the extent of white colouration in the throat, for example) to be able to tell them apart. But you have to do that between the males of the species, too.

A name, after all, is only a category label; and an

eponym – in this case that of a nineteenth-century vicar from Durham – is only more useful than a descriptive name in its brevity. But naming a species after a female feature might just help redress the balance a bit, and perhaps it could also help change the way we look, and what we notice.

Another approach could be to recognise some of those who have been overlooked, such as Gemil. The very process of my questioning whether Tristram still deserves (or ever deserved) to be honoured with an eponym feels like an inadvertent assertion of his claim to importance, and it risks crowding out those like Gemil, even though they have at least an equal right to be recognised and honoured. The Bird Names for Birds campaign group states that eponyms 'are essentially verbal statues' which embody colonial exploits and the racist structures that enabled them, but perhaps renaming birds to honour individuals or groups erased by those acts would help create a different kind of verbal statue, one that brings to light people who have been excluded.

A photograph of Tristram taken in Durham depicts him dressed in his full Middle East travel outfit and sporting a well-kept hipster beard. Where the bird-heist boys have baseball caps, he has a Foreign Legion

Sahara kepi, and where they have binoculars he has his most precious bit of gear, his rifle, highlighting the tenuous boundary in the nineteenth century between hunting and collecting, between shooting for pleasure and 'obtaining' specimens for the benefit of science. Tristram lamented damage done to his gun. Early in 1864, while exploring a wadi near the Dead Sea, he shot a Palestine sunbird and a fantail warbler – but, as he reported: 'I also unfortunately signalised the morning by falling down a rock, and bruising not only myself, but – what was of more consequence – my gun, an injury here irreparable.' The theft of his opera glass a couple of months later was, by contrast, only 'an irreparable loss in bird-nesting' – and by 'bird-nesting' he meant locating and raiding birds' nests for his egg collection.

While the bird-heist portrait of birdwatchers as heroic adventurers in 2019 is evidently a knowing joke about the stereotype of the nerdy birder, there does not appear to be anything self-deprecating or humorous in the portrait of Tristram posing heroically in his explorer regalia. It expresses quite vividly the complex history and Western imperial values that make honorific bird names so problematic.

The pose in which he stands in that old photograph looks absurd now, though it was no doubt a serious matter at the time. I wish I could believe there was the same element of self-satire that is evident in the bird-heist boys' portrait. But the evidence, from Tristram's writing, is that he was a zealous and often derogatory guardian of his own reputation, sniping at those who questioned his authority, particularly his authority on the birds of Palestine.

Sadly, despite the knowing and self-deprecating humour in the bird-heist boys' photograph, subsequent events have changed how it looks. One of the individuals was summarily fired by various bird groups and organisations with which he was affiliated, after he was accused by a fellow birdwatcher of sexual assault. That development rather highlights the absence of women birdwatchers, both in the original image and in the photoshopped versions which added explosions but no bird-heist girl.

I think of the many contemporary ornithological adventurers revealed during #BlackBirdersWeek – the images of girls and women in their natural research habitat, up to their waists in swamps, up to their elbows in samples, and in one memorable case, a lively video of a girl belaying her brother on a crag, chattering excitedly about seeing her first peregrine. And then I think of the girl whom Tristram described in 1865, when he and his companions were trying to raid a griffon vulture nest in Wady Hamam, where the cliffs, 'reaching the height of 1,500 feet, rise like terraces, with enormous masses of debris.' Some of his companions abseiled down or were lowered on ropes to reach the nests, 'while those above were guided in working them by signals from others below in the valley.... The idea of scaling these cliffs with ropes was quite new to some Arabs who were herding cattle above, and who could not, excepting one little girl, be induced to render any assistance. She proved herself most nimble and efficient in telegraphing.' The girl remained unnamed, though Tristram evidently met her, because he described how she had a piercing of a type he'd never seen before: 'instead of nose-rings, a turquoise pin-head was fastened through the flesh, flat to the nose, on each side of her nostrils.'

Tristram and his fellow collectors 'reaped a good harvest of griffons' eggs' on that occasion, raiding fourteen nests, but birds weren't all that Tristram observed from that height. He also watched a Muslim funeral below him. The body was 'stripped, laid on a board, and, while the women washed it, and stuffed the eyes, ears, mouth, and nose with cotton-wool, the men dug a grave. It was then buried, without further ceremony or covering, and the whole party, having yelled two or three times, "There is one God, and

Mohammed is His prophet," filled up the grave under a bush, and returned.' Limited as he was by his own English Anglican ignorance, Tristram couldn't keep himself from exclaiming: 'Poor creatures! dark and ignorant they live, and so they die.'

9. The Promise of Puffins

I miscalculated how long it would take to drive to Marloes Head. We were already late, when round the bend of the narrow high-hedged road towards the headland, we fetched up behind a flock of sheep. My tension squeezed tighter. The later we were, the longer we'd have to queue for the Skomer Island ferry; if there were a lot of people, we might not make it onto a ferry at all. I knew the sheep would add at most ten minutes to the journey, but everything had been a rush that morning: we'd set off without breakfast and we were still going to have to stop for coffee and something to eat, which would make us later yet. Now the world had slowed to the pace of recalcitrant ewes, while my mind raced round and round a closed circuit of stress.

My mother had travelled all the way from Australia to see me and we had done almost nothing I'd promised her we could do. I was working three part-time jobs that spilled over into her visit; I was broke, and hadn't been able to refuse a freelance project that came my way. The plan for a few days in the Lake District, where she'd never been, dissipated before my new deadline and growing overdraft. Walks up Cadair Idris or Snowdon had shrunk to walks at Cors Caron or up on the common. But the experience of puffins on Skomer was non-negotiable. She might go back to Queensland without ever seeing Snowdon or Skiddaw or Scafell Pike, but she wasn't going home without seeing puffins.

At last the sheep peeled off into their new field, and I charged on, stopping briefly at a café in Marloes itself for coffee, a sticky brownie, and the loo, swearing at slow tourists (because everyone visiting a tourist site is a tourist except for me), and trying to ignore the dashboard clock. At last we turned into the car park near the ferry terminal. To my surprise and relief, it was nearly empty. It looked as if there might not be a queue for the ferry after all. But I was wrong. There was a sign near the kiosk: all the boat crossings had been cancelled because of the high wind.

The relief of tension was so sudden that I felt for a moment blank and confused. This failure, at least, was not of my doing: it was out of my hands.

My mother manages disappointment well – or she

hides it well. She shrugged, pragmatic and amused. It was still a beautiful place to walk, that rocky Pembrokeshire headland; we could still see Skomer, and maybe we'd see puffins from the mainland, and other seabirds. It was spring; the wildflowers were bright and varied and as interesting to her as birds.

We parked, and got out, and walked over to take a look at the sandwich board that listed recent ornithological sightings. It's a prime migration spot, and it was May, a good time to see scarcer visitors. Top of the morning's birds was a really exciting listing: a female golden oriole – which is to say, more accurately, a green oriole. My mother pointed at it and looked at me, and I knew we were both remembering the golden oriole we'd heard and briefly glimpsed in France when I was a child, an experience that was memorable as much for the unanticipated discovery as for the delight of the melodious and unmistakable song.

Perhaps, I hoped, desperately, if she saw that golden oriole it would make up for the puffins. Everything else that I'd planned had gone awry; she'd come so far to explore new places with me, and I'd repeatedly let her down. And worse: my stress had made me scratchy, irritable; I had been bad company, impatient and reactive. But at least she could enjoy the Pembrokeshire sea cliffs. Maybe we'd glimpse the oriole; maybe out to sea we'd see gannets diving over some shoal of fish, and then the porpoises that so often accompany them. And there were the wildflowers: she could wander and stop and look as much as she liked. I would get my aggravated stress under control, and not think about work, or deadlines, or how I was going to pay my bills. I'd be better company.

It was a beautiful, clear, breezy day, with the kind of high wind that makes horses agitated, the kind of day when cows race about comically, though if you're a heifer, there's nothing entertaining about a gadfly that wants to get her eggs into your digestive tract ('the cows were on the gad,' TH White wrote in *The Once and Future King*, 'and could be seen galloping about with their tails in the air' – once read, that book is always a once and future association).

I understand why it unsettles horses and cattle, that kind of hot sky and high wind. It unsettled me, as though something was about to happen. I used to feel the same thing during earthquake weather – the hot, still days in the San Francisco Bay Area which have no connection to earthquakes, but which cause the same kind of agitated anticipation, like the first hit of caffeine.

As I read down the bird sightings list, I understood,

with dread, what that sense of something imminent had presaged. A blank appeared in my vision on the left: a nothingness, a hole. I looked away at the parked cars, and the nothingness looked with me: it blanked out the registration plate of a car on the left. 'Fuck,' I said out loud. 'Fuck, fuck, *fuck*.'

'What is it?' my mother asked, confused.

'Blind spot,' I said. 'I've got a blind spot. I'm getting a migraine.'

I knew what would follow, as she knew what would follow: we respond to stress – or, more specifically, the lifting of stress – in similar ways. It would be there for about twenty minutes, that blind spot in the left of my vision; it would grow, and then a little jagged, jerky, garish circle of ugly light would start jiggling about and expand and spread to surround my entire left field of vision, zig-zagging in harsh electric colours, inescapable, whether my eyes were open or shut. While it was there I would not be able to do anything but lie down. After an hour it would slow, dull a little, become diffuse and gradually fade away. Then the profound nausea would begin, and finally the headache, which might last a day, or two, along with a cognitive slowness, like jetlag.

Migraines don't happen spontaneously. It wasn't

the sudden weight of failure, when I learned that the ferries were cancelled, and all of the ways I'd let my mother down descended on me – nor the relief from the stress that something out of my hands had decided things for me. The conditions had been set earlier. The brownie had been a sign, just as the sense of imminence had been a sign, but I'd missed it, because I'd misunderstood it. A desire for chocolate was a symptom, though at that point I thought it must be the cause, and as a result the association between chocolate and migraine became so marked that afterwards I never again ate chocolate. The cancelled ferry, the strange release from responsibility, was only a final tipping point. The migraine had been set in motion anyway by the fear that I could not make my mother's visit worth her while, even if we went to Skomer.

The truth is, it wasn't only that it was out of my hands, that release from stress. I hadn't really wanted to go to Skomer. I'd been once, years before, and once was enough. If you take the boat in the breeding season you know you are not only guaranteed to see a puffin – you are guaranteed to see dozens of puffins at close quarters. To miss seeing puffins you would have to focus exclusively on the Manx shearwater corpses that litter the paths, the birds killed and partially eaten by waiting great black-backed gulls.

The puffins emerge from their burrows, all clown face and bright beak, and they are a comical, endearing, trundling delight. But I am ambivalent about that delight. It's as though they are being made to perform for us, the spectators, and they put on a good show, particularly for the ranks of men with enormous extended lenses who line up along the paths.

Cameras more than binoculars have become the signature of a particular subspecies of obsessive birdwatcher. It's not just 'pics or it didn't happen' that drives the bird photographers with their ever larger and more powerful cameras and scopes. Nor is the display of personal gear in itself a problem: it's what they do with it. On Skomer, the photographers behaved as though the puffins were there for them. They stepped off the paths, lay down in the heather with a camera trained on a burrow, getting between birds and their nests for a close-up shot that had been done hundreds or probably thousands of times. But it doesn't matter that your image is like a thousand other images: this is *your* shot; it is you who's got this bird in the bag.

Some bird photographers will willingly and illegally disturb protected nest sites for the sake of a close shot. An RSPB officer on Mull told me that one photographer's guide had been handed ASBOs for his persistent, reckless violation of the law against disturbing the nest sites of rare birds. These days, obsessive or thoughtless bird photographers are a greater risk than egg thieves to the island's great wildlife tourist attraction, the white-tailed eagle.

The white-tailed eagle is purportedly Britain's third-rarest breeding raptor. I wonder, though, about the two rarer species, honey buzzards and Montagu's harriers, and whether there might not be others that only an elite few know about – the one-off nest of a pallid harrier, say, which gets passed off as a similar-looking hen harrier to the unknowing. It's not just because of egg thieves and criminally inclined gamekeepers that rare raptors' nests are closely guarded secrets.

I hadn't gone to Mull to see white-tailed eagles, though I had hoped to see one when I was there. But I'd been as uneasy about the eagle spectacle as I was about the puffins on Skomer. You can get up close to a white-tailed eagle on a boat trip, when they come obediently for the bait that the boat operators throw out for them, or you can visit one of the RSPB's nest sites, but I wanted to see one by chance, by paying attention – not by paying for a tourist experience.

Mull wildlife has been packaged as one of its great tourist attractions, and it has been promoted as a great photography opportunity, too, because these days your experiences have to be validated by Instagram. Visitors' accounts and photographs of sightings, *Spring Watch* and tourist agencies and self-catering cottage booking websites seem to suggest that if you so much as step outside, you'll see an eagle whizzing past, if you're not tripping over an otter.

'The hair will go up on the back of your neck,' the writer Niall Griffiths said to me, when I told him I was going to Mull, and that I hoped I might see white-tailed eagles. He'd gone out on one of the boat trips; he, like everyone to whom I mentioned the birds, used a 'flying barn door' comparison to try to convey the impact of the eagle's size and bulk. But when I thought of a barn I could not visualise what a barn door looked like, let alone one in flight. Surely, I thought, the characteristic of a barn was that it didn't have doors – 'Were you born in a barn?' you used to get asked, if you left a door open.

Despite my anticipation, there were no white-tailed eagles, nor any otters, even though there are otter-crossing signs warning drivers to slow down. It's a strangely superstitious state of mind you get into, when you want to see something, but you don't want to jinx seeing it. You look, all the time – scanning sky and sere hillside and the water's edge, scanning all the time – looking, looking *for*, but at the same time also looking slant, as though you will frighten what you might see by looking at it directly, even though you haven't seen it yet.

My puritanical code about a chance sighting was self-defeating. I didn't even know that the general location of a nest site was loudly proclaimed by bright yellow 'Eagle Watch' and CCTV warning signs and 'Absolutely No Parking' injunctions. I just hadn't been in the right place to see the signs. In the end, feeling unclean, I succumbed: I paid for one of the RSPB's nest site visits.

We gathered at the designated meeting place by a track leading from the road. There were eight cars, waiting for the arrival of Debbie, the RSPB ranger, who led us up a few hundred metres into a forestry tract. We parked in a clearing near a temporary roofed shelter with three telescopes set up on tripods. Inconveniently, white-tailed eagles might maintain several nest sites, and there's no guarantee which they will choose to use each year, so the public RSPB nest-watches have to be somewhat mobile.

The nest site was no inaccessible cliff-top eyrie, the kind of locale that lends all the poetic romanticism to the eagle in a mountain fastness, but a mere hundred metres from the road. It was a branchy tangle near the top of a conifer at the edge of a clear-cut slope. Not far from the nest, loggers were felling trees, but the birds were used to it.

One of the group unpacked camera and lenses from a case. He ignored all the small chatter of the amateurs – his was evidently a serious purpose. Intent and uncommunicative, he prepared his gear and waited, camera poised. He didn't have to wait long. The female was on the nest, and after two false alarms when she sat up calling – a buzzard both times – the male arrived, flying over us and then in front of us. He landed in a tree beside the nest, allowing us a slow and luxurious examination of his massiveness. More like a vulture than an eagle, I thought – something about its heaviness and the flatness of its flight reminded me of the griffon vultures of my childhood visits to Israel. Perhaps this was what was meant by the 'flying barn door' analogy, though I still could not visualise what a barn door might look like.

'Did you get it?' the photographer's partner asked. He nodded, expressionless. Another man in a tight nylon checked shirt buttoned to the throat wanted to know whether we would also be able to see a golden eagle. Possibly, he was told, but there was no guarantee. So he left. The sighting of the white-tailed eagle didn't seem to have pleased him or the photographer very much.

To me too it seemed somehow unsatisfactory, and inconclusive. I'd seen a white-tailed eagle, but I did not *feel* as if I'd really seen one, not authentically – not until one flew over unexpectedly close, near Duart Castle. Then, under the shadow of that huge predator, for an instant I found myself flinching and ducking in an instinct to make myself small and invisible, and for a long time afterwards, my heart raced.

My mother didn't see the rare oriole – and she didn't go looking for it; she didn't need it. While I lay down in the car with a coat over my head, and waited for the worst part of my migraine to subside, she wandered for a happy hour exploring the wildflowers. After my eyesight returned to normal, I got out of the car and went to find her. We sat together on the rabbit-bitten headland among the thrift, taking in the sound and smell of the sea breaking at the foot of the cliffs, saying very little. Maybe there were puffins passing further out, towards the island of Grassholm, but it somehow didn't seem to matter so much anymore. All my stress was gone, my mind stilled in the aftermath of the small seizure that is a migraine. The blank spot and the jagged aura were gone, but the nausea and the headache meant that I could not look. It was the quietest, easiest time we spent in the three weeks of her visit – not looking, but being: enough, I hoped, to make up for what we might have missed.

10. To Gawp at Birds

Travelling by train from Birmingham to Aberystwyth is possibly the only time I feel an affinity with fellow birdwatchers, perhaps the only time I recognise them in any way as 'fellow' anything. Though there may not be any binoculars in sight, you can tell who they are because of what they pay attention to out of the window, or whether they pay attention at all.

Halfway along the route, the train stops for fifteen minutes at Shrewsbury. Many people change trains here, and as they leave, some of the remaining passengers move to seats facing back the way they came. When the train departs, seeming to reverse its course, those who are making the journey for the first time clutch their bags and sit up, startled, looking out the window and around them, thinking they're on the way back to Birmingham, wondering what they've missed, until someone in the know takes pity and explains, or the bilingual announcement of the next stop, over the border in Welshpool, reassures them. Then they sit back again, let go of their bags, take a drink of water, resume the conversations they were having on their phones.

But among those who have changed seats in Shrewsbury I always notice the birdwatchers; they will have claimed new forward-facing window seats on the right-hand side of the carriage. From there they'll have a view, when the time comes, of the river and estuary over which the RSPB's Ynys-hir hides look – and, before that, a view of the raised platform of branches where the Dyfi ospreys nest in the Montgomeryshire Wildlife Trust reserve.

Early on, when the Dyfi Osprey Project had successfully attracted ospreys back to nest in mid Wales for the first time in some 300 years, train conductors used to make an announcement during the breeding season as the train approached the nest near Dyfi Junction. It used to remind me of a California bus driver who would declare heavily, as we headed north out of Oakland, 'Now entering the People's Republic of Berkeley.'

Ospreys are spectacular birds and, like Skomer's puffins, they always put on a good show. Their nesting habits lend themselves to the conservation spectacle that they've become – both on the Dyfi, and further north in the Glaslyn valley, and at long-established sites in England and Scotland. The nest is a highly visible heap of dead branches in a suitable tree (or, as is the case on the Dyfi, on a specially built platform), and unlike white-tailed eagles they return to the same nest site, displacing presumptuous interlopers.

The spectacle of the Dyfi Osprey Project is available twenty-four hours a day during the nesting season. You can watch the show on your phone, your tablet, your TV screen, or you can watch it from the purpose-built 360-degree observatory, with its telescopes, livestream screens, information boards and displays, along with easy parking, convenient loos, and a café and gift shop. It makes a pleasant day out; the staff are knowledgeable and welcoming; the birds are impressive and also beautiful, and you're guaranteed to see at least one. In a good breeding year, after the young have fledged, you might see as many as five ospreys at one go, from the train window or the observatory.

The Dyfi osprey nest was a novelty to start with; now it's a huge tourist attraction, a wild spectacle. An osprey pair raising young is a dramatic story, and the public following of the webcams on the nest grows at a phenomenal rate year on year, in large part because the staff at the reserve have made the ospreys so accessible. There are plenty of nest livestreams around the world, but the way the ospreys are presented through the Trust's website, their blogs, and on social media has captivated the public. Naming individual birds and the young they raise has also personalised the ospreys of the Dyfi.

Originally frequented by a single male, the nest that the Trust erected is sometimes now the contested site of several ospreys in the early breeding season, which adds tension and drama for those caught up in the story of their return each spring. Their mating, their nest-making, the female's egg-laying, the hatching, their raising of young, the young's fledging, and their departure at the end of summer and in early autumn is all caught on livestream. It's an unfolding spectacle that is followed day by day, hour by hour (and, near hatching or fledging time, minute by minute) by thousands of watchers and commentators and visitors, who make a soap opera out of the ospreys, projecting every human attribute imaginable onto individuals and whole species, from uncontrolled amorousness to evil, murderous intent. The birds have been anthropomorphised beyond retrieval by the public, even if the Trust staff do so only in a light-hearted, humorous manner (there's a virtual self-imposed fine of 50p in the commentary or blogs every time a member of staff or the public strays into overt anthropomorphism).

For nature writers, it seems hardly a question that anthropomorphism is anathema. Of a description of swifts by Gilbert White in his eighteenth-century classic, *The Natural History of Selborne*, Richard Mabey writes: 'With no more than a hint of anthropomorphism, White suggests that their lives have a richness and rhythm of their own.' Whatever it is that constitutes nature writing, what it cannot, must not be is anthropomorphic. In this case, apparently White just skims the edge of that pit of iniquity. More recently, in the vibrantly written *The Screaming Sky,* Charles Foster excoriates anthropomorphic and anthropocentric approaches to understanding swifts, or any wild thing. To him, writers who do it both denigrate and domesticate. 'Why do you want the swifts, Mr Loxdale?' he asks, after quoting a particularly anthropocentric poem. 'To reassure you that the world is still turning smoothly, so that you can get on with your life?' The *Screaming Sky* is peppered with absolute assertions about proper attitudes. 'Don't patronise,' he announces, patronising his reader (aggravated, I find myself wanting to do precisely what I'm told not to do just to spite him).

I wonder whether anthropomorphising is, in itself, such an iniquitous thing. Everybody does it, even if we try to keep it private. At least I think everyone does it; I certainly do, though I know I shouldn't (but 'shouldn't' according to whom, I wonder, picturing Foster tutting and wagging his finger at me).

I think of the photographs by a friend of mine who recently discovered birdwatching and bird photography. He delights in the most accessible common birds, and on social media he posts sharp images that capture their consistent and unmistakable attitudes – the unassuming dunnock, the cocky wren, the goggle-eyed woodpigeon. Of course I know birds don't have attitudes: they have *behaviour*. The woodpigeon is not demented; the wren is not cocky; the dunnock is no more unassuming than a robin is presumptuous. I know this kind of projection of human attributes onto wild birds is, to some birdwatching and nature writing purists, a failing of sorts, an unfortunate display of ignorance. If you don't conform to the convention of scientifically objective language you lose credibility as an observer. Nevertheless, despite the conventions and my best intentions, I can only apprehend the world within the limitations of my own human cognition, my particular ways of relating. I recognise the value of trying to apprehend the natural world in other than human terms, but that, too, is a human, value-laden approach, which requires human, value-laden choices; it is not an absolute good, in itself; it does not intrinsically lead to more commendable behaviour. Perhaps in this, as in so many areas of contention over 'correct' attitudes, what really matters is not how you think, but how you act.

To be fair, trying not to fall into the trap of an anthropocentric view of the natural world is an act as well as a thought – an act that at least seeks to avoid perpetuating some of the damage done by a paternalistic and exploitative attitude. But even as a conservation effort such as the Dyfi Osprey Project seeks to repair human damage, it seems by its spectacular nature to reinforce rather than challenge an anthropomorphic and anthropocentric attitude, whatever the concerted efforts by its staff to remind the public of such errors. Maybe that in itself is not a problem, except that the conservation spectacle, like the zoo, demands nothing of you. To be a spectator of birds can be an act of consumption equivalent to the pleasure of the slice of cake and cup of coffee you enjoy afterwards.

What 'should' someone take away from looking at ospreys (and 'should' according to whom – to me)?

What should it demand of an individual visitor? Must everyone struggle here too, as in nature writing, with the story of ecocide, as Mark Cocker implicitly asserted back in 2014 when he objected to the failure of the then 'new' nature writing to demand that the reader engage with the story of 'bulldozing our fellow Britons – between 60,000 and 80,000 species of animal and plant – over the cliff into oblivion'?

The conservation project has lured ospreys back to mid Wales, and they now also breed in other less well-known locations nearby. Its environmental impact is considerable. But how valuable is the conservation spectacle to the public if, afterwards, you go on buying new to replace old when repairing old will do; drop rubbish because someone else will clean it up; fly frequently for brief holidays; spray your garden with herbicides and pesticides, or concrete it all over and lay plastic grass that will degrade and make its way, as microplastics, into watercourses – in short, change nothing about how you interact with the natural world except adding a line of heart emojis to a comment on the Dyfi Osprey Project's Facebook post?

The way I ask that question is also implicitly to presume to answer it, in a way that differs very little from the judgements I object to myself – the exclusive claim on knowing what is the right attitude to take to swifts, for example, or the proper purpose and method of experiencing the wild. There is more than one way to understand the human relationship to other species, to the natural environment; there is more than one kind of relationship.

Maybe some people, after seeing the Dyfi ospreys, do go home unchanged, but maybe for some the Dyfi osprey spectacle is a gateway to engage further with the natural world – even if they don't engage with the less delightful drama of its imminent oblivion. Maybe it is only an online soap opera to some, but to others those distant birds might be the first ones they've ever noticed; maybe they begin to notice other birds, too, and rivers, and news stories about water companies releasing effluent, or slurry run-off that kills osprey food.

I might cringe at commodification of the natural world, and the anthropomorphism of a wild bird, and I might view the easy consumption of spectacle with something approaching derision, comfortable in my own purism, but is the attitude of birdwatchers, or my own attitude, any better? I imagine that certain kinds of birdwatchers would rarely visit that observatory to look at ospreys, because to them (and to me) the guaranteed sighting is not what birdwatching is really about. Though I've visited, reluctantly, I'd be uneasy about going back, the way I was uneasy about going back to Skomer with my mother.

My puritanical code dictates that seeing a rare bird by guarantee, laid on as spectacle, is a cheat: it's inauthentic. The birdwatcher purist in me says that a chance sight of an osprey going over my house, as happened once, or of a golden eagle skimming along below me after I toiled up the 3,000-foot ascent of Ben More on Mull is somehow ethical, whereas the guaranteed sight of an osprey on the Dyfi nest, or a white-tailed eagle at the RSPB nest watch in the Tioran woodland, or dozens of puffins by the path on Skomer, all entail a kind of laziness. Because the former results from chance, or effort with no guarantee of a reward, and is unmediated by others – and because it also relies on my own skill at identification – it feels worth something, while the latter offers an assured outcome that feels unearned.

I know I'm not alone in this, but it's slightly disorientating to see my own puritan attitude articulated by others. 'Simply watching nature on the CCTV screen is inferred as a passive act as opposed to a skill, which for the more serious bird-watcher is deemed as a lesser, inferior mode of engagement,' reports the author of a study published in 2007. Back then, CCTV rather than a web livestream was the innovative tech used for surveillance of a nest, and for attracting more human visitors. A volunteer at an RSPB site told the study's author that those kinds of birdwatchers 'actually want to go out and find it for themselves.... I think it comes down to, a lot of them see it as cheating....'

But there's something else at stake in this purism, too. If 68 million people suddenly wanted to experience in a direct way the sovereign otherness of the wild places or species of the UK, untrammelled by the mediation of reserves and interpretation boards, accessible paths and nest-cams, and the presence of other humans, it would be something that no one could experience. By its nature, a direct and unmediated experience of the wild can only be accessed by a few, or it ceases to be that experience. Instead it becomes common, in both senses of the word. The 'proper' experience of the wild, for the purist, is valued in proportion to its inaccessibility – just as the sighting of a scarce bird is in part valued in proportion to how few can see it.

Perhaps the fundamental appeal of all collecting – whether trainspotting or birdwatching or the now illegal egg-collecting – lies in the pleasure of owning or experiencing something exclusive. At the Dyfi Osprey Project, as on Skomer, I feel reduced to being a bird tourist, a consumer of bird spectacle: I become a spectator in a crowd. If an experience is common, it's not special. If anyone can see this particular rare bird, it takes something away from its rarity. Perhaps, properly, there are really two forms of rarity, and associated value: the numerical scarcity of the bird itself, and the rare experience of seeing a scarce bird. It's this latter form that is threatened by the popular bird conservation spectacle, just as popular forms of writing about the natural world threaten special ownership of and authority about wild experience. If anyone can have this experience, it might not be worth having.

There are more troubling implications in these hierarchies of value than the dubious pleasures of corralling to yourself what is precious. The puritan code of purported authenticity relies on exclusion. Not everyone who wants to see an osprey (or a white-tailed eagle, or puffins) has the same access as I have to a chance encounter. I have leisure, physical mobility, reasonably good eyesight and hearing, a private means of transport, and access to many other resources that I take so much for granted that I hardly recognise them. All of those unacknowledged resources give me a freedom to have some notionally more 'real' or authentic experience than the shared experience in the

Dyfi Osprey Observatory, or on the flat maintained paths on Skomer, or in an RSPB hide with a wheelchair ramp. But my private moment of encounter is not more authentic than a shared one. It is the result of many invisible privileges – that weighty, over-burdened word – that not everyone has. The judgement that says, even if only secretly, that it is more real, or more authentic than, say, a child for the first time seeing an osprey from an observatory, is simply an expression of exclusivity and implicit hostility – as is dictating the 'right' attitude to take to swifts, or the 'proper' approach to take in nature writing.

It's threatening to open up the boundaries of your group to include others who might not share your values or attitudes, because to do so might change the nature of your experience. It can be the case with any group, notional or real. I, for one, don't want to change. Sullenly I resist the idea that the value and authenticity of an experience that I care about is based on my enjoying certain privileges. They don't feel like privileges – but then privilege never does feel like privilege: experientially it is always relative, not absolute. There is always someone else you can point to who has more advantages than you, as though this somehow diminishes or even cancels out your own advantages.

Like a child in nursery clutching their toy that another child wants to play with, I stubbornly try to hold on to my sense of what is authentic and valuable. The teacherly argument that if we all share, we all gain, because we (meaning me, if I share) get to play with other people's toys, too, means nothing to a three-year-old. I don't want to play with other people's toys. I'm not interested in anyone else's toys. I want to play with my own toy, and I don't want anyone else to touch it, or use it, or even look at it, because if they do that, it won't be special anymore; it won't be *mine* anymore. And worse: it would be sullied. It's precious because you want it and can't have it; because I have it, and you don't.

I want to hold on to the belief that birdwatching 'in the field', and participating in the laid-on bird spectacle at a reserve, are fundamentally different in value, though both involve looking at birds. But there's another aspect of the conservation spectacle that also makes me uneasy. It forces me to confront something unpalatable about the nature of birdwatching itself, which is that I watch for my own pleasure and gratification. There's no getting around the fact. It makes no difference morally whether I am seeing a bird that I'm guaranteed to see by virtue of others' intervention, or whether I'm seeing a bird by chance or by some kind of effort. The delusion of it somehow being earned does not change the act of looking, or the pleasure of watching without being watched.

The shared experience of watching birds might make me feel like a spectator, but the private experience of watching birds makes me a voyeur. Mark Cocker seems to deny this voyeurism even as he acknowledges it. In his taxonomy of people interested in birds, he objects both to the terms 'bird-watcher' (because of what he deems the redundant hyphen) and the unhyphenated 'birdwatcher', proposing that, 'even as a single word, "birdwatcher" sounds so passive and voyeuristic that you'd probably be far more disinclined to take it up.' And yet both terms – maybe the first even more so – describe unambiguously what is going on: looking at birds is a voyeuristic activity. Cocker's preference for the term 'birding', which, to him, suggests 'the appropriate depth of identification between observer and his subject', elides that voyeurism, with its social stigma of the Peeping Tom who is gratified by intruding on privacy, who is thrilled by watching without being seen.

Acknowledging a voyeuristic sexual preference is evidently socially taboo, but it seems that for Cocker the pursuit of sexual conquest, by contrast, carries no such shame. The language he uses to explain his bird obsession is repeatedly sexual, whether it's about binoculars (described in terms of marriage, bigamy and promiscuity), about bird notebooks (adultery, clandestine relationships), or about the more focused pursuit of rare birds. 'I was happy to risk my ornitho-virginity,' he reports, of sighting an Iceland gull for the first time. 'I was fourteen. She – so to speak – was eighteen.' For him, 'seeing this ghostly bird for the first time bordered on the orgasmic.' But it's not just for him that birding is sexual. He recounts one birder 'announcing after seeing one particular rarity, "It were so good I nearly creamed me pants." That robust male directness gets to the nub of the matter. Birds can be erotic.' Even if some of his sexual language might be intended as humour, that conclusion is definitive: there is nothing socially embarrassing about acknowledging the hunting and conquest element of watching birds.

Like most women, I am used to being looked at by straight men, and being assessed not as an individual but as a set of physical attributes of greater or lesser interest. Women are watched, and are pursued as sexual quarry, and it's surely no accident that in English the noun 'bird' should be applied to us, both in dismissal (just some bird) and as possession (*my* bird). So for me the term *birding* is both more assertively sexual and more disingenuous than the voyeurism in *birdwatching*, even if *birding* might be preferable as an acknowledgement that the visual is not the only way to encounter birds.

I might snigger at the phallic over-compensation of competitive male birders (both in their gear and their language), but all birdwatching – theirs or mine; the secret glimpse while privately skulking, or the shared public spectacle – is voyeuristic in an uncomfortably suggestive way. The act of watching for pleasure – sexual or otherwise – is human, and we shape that experience with human language. No matter how uncomfortable it is to acknowledge, there's no escaping the anthropocentrism that determines how we approach birds, and the natural world more generally, nor the anthropomorphism with which we understand and describe what we see.

The logical outcome to this discomfort about what birdwatching actually entails might be to forego the pleasure of looking at all. But I'm not going to forego that pleasure. I'm not sure I could, even if I tried. Once you begin to notice birds (after a visit to the Dyfi observatory, say), it's hard to unnotice them, no matter where it occurs, or what moral anxiety you bring to it. Besides, acting on that logical outcome would just be absurd and pointless self-aggrandisement. It would certainly have no impact on birds.

11. The Regard of Equals

Outside the kitchen window, in front of the house, a blackbird with a dirty beak eyes me eyeing him. He's been digging into the leaf litter, and some of the residue has stuck. He looks from one eye and then turns his head and looks from the other. Then he cocks his head, looking high up at something else. He looks at me again, and takes off for the ridge of the roof above me, out of sight, and I feel the usual letdown, the regret, that I have been the cause of fear.

I wonder about looking at birds, whether they feel watched, whether they know but carry on anyway. Does the watcher register like an anxious background mutter, a feeling of threat that is not yet identified, not yet acted on? The whole effort of people obsessed with birds is to see without being seen, else you would see precious little – but even so, for me the moment that really counts is when the bird I'm looking at looks back at me, makes an assessment, and carries on, unafraid: when I manage to convey that I am no threat. If it takes off, as this blackbird took off, my regret is the regret of an exchange that went awry – because I meant no harm and posed no threat.

Then I hear the blackbird's clucking alarm call behind the house, and I open the back door to an early morning hubbub. A brown shape is flailing around in the brambles at the edge of the wood, and a wren, a nuthatch, and a blackcap are giving loud opinions and warnings from nearby. I think a buzzard has caught something, is struggling on the ground with prey rather larger or stronger than it counted on.

I pull on my boots and tramp out. It's disappeared, but there is a commotion under the brambles, and a complex squeaking that is no bird, no rabbit caught in talons. When I come near, the squeaking falls silent, the commotion stops, and then out from the brambles two polecats emerge. One, much smaller, slips away down the bank to the shed and in through a hole where the panel has come loose. The other, bulkier, masked, stands in the path a metre away and looks at me for a long moment.

Then for a moment I am afraid.

I'm ashamed of my fear, in all the forms it takes. It seems like a terrible weakness. It enrages me to remember how cowed I used to be, how afraid I was, enrages me that I should ever have been made to feel that way, that any woman should feel that way – and yet when I see it in another woman, my rage turns on her, not on the man who's got her under his control.

I recognise it in other women instantly, the way I might recognise a known bird. At least I *think* I do. I would not be able to say what, precisely, I rely on – what features, what visual or aural or scent markers, what posture or plumage or movement come together in a moment's impression to tell me *domestic abuse*, but I know it with what both the components of the word 'recognition' suggest: a previous knowledge re-experienced. And with that recognition comes a miserable rage.

When we lived together, I used to fantasise wildly, intemperately about his death – his death in a train crash, in a terrorist attack, in an earthquake. I didn't wish him pain, or suffering; it's not that I wished him dead. I just fantasised about an escape through disaster for which I was not responsible, the only escape that was possible. Because even if I left him, it would not end. Not because he would pursue me, or threaten me, but because he would continue to exist, would continue to judge me and be angry, and I would be abject all my life. My life would be shaped by trying to repudiate that judgement, or appease that anger. He would never not matter, because he knew me, and I could only be free of his anger and judgement in his approval, which I could not ever earn.

In fear of his anger I externalised approval, like a child. I sought his approval, and, seeking it, accepted that I could never have it, because seeking it made me abject, and therefore not worthy of it. As petitioner, I re-established precisely what I wished to undo. This was the trap from which the only escape was actual escape.

In my waking life I fantasised about a disaster that would provide my escape; in my sleep I dreamed of the aftermath of disaster, which was the huge cost of escape. I dreamed terrible repeat scenes of war, of death camps, of the devastating earthquake that was always still to come. All communication would be down, and I'd find a public phone but it would be missing some of its buttons, so that I could not dial 911, or 999, or it would turn out that it was not a phone but a calculator; or I would find the phone cord had been torn from the box, its end frayed. It would be a phone box in an urban street, gum-encrusted, stinking of urine, full of broken glass and detritus – or the phone box would be empty: there was, simply, no means of communication, no way to ask for help, for rescue.

And when I woke, I would realise that I had to update our emergency numbers, that I had to do an earthquake drill; I needed to buy water treatment tablets, and replace the old tins I'd put aside in the earthquake supplies box on the front porch. I would lie there in the flood of waking relief, haunted still by disaster, in wonder at my mind's capacity to remind me of my responsibilities, to remind me of jobs not done, of the denial that everyone in earthquake country lives with. For to be prepared for an earthquake – which, then, years ago, meant keeping a radio with charged batteries; enough food and water for three days; blankets, torches, the tool for the gas shut-off – requires that you confront the real, definite future earthquake on the Hayward or San Andreas Fault, not some time in the next ten or thirty years but imminent; not the possibility or probability but the certainty of it. And to do that is to confront an impending disaster, at which your first and strongest reaction is not to prepare, but to escape. It sets in train an impossible sequence of thought: that you cannot live in this dangerous place, you must move, but you cannot act immediately. You cannot quit your job and pack up and go elsewhere in that moment of urgency, and so it becomes less urgent, and then it quiets a bit into something to think and talk about, and then settles into something to put off, so that again, in a matter of mere moments, an imminent disaster from which you must escape becomes a set of tasks you ought to see to, but don't, or which you begin and never finish. 'We should review our earthquake plan,' you might say that night over dinner; or, in the supermarket that afternoon, you might select six tins of beans, or new batteries. And soon enough, when everyone's ill and the house hasn't much food, or you can't be bothered to cook, you open one of the tins and heat up the beans, and don't replace the tin; and then, needing batteries, you raid your incomplete, scattered, poorly organised and out-of-date earthquake supplies, and don't think about replacing them until the next dream of catastrophe.

At no time did I confront what all the dreams were really telling me: they were not about the dangers I lived in, the muttering, raw background of my fear, the labyrinth of his rage, but the danger that I posed to myself. I could not face my desire for escape, because I would have had to act on it, and be responsible for the consequences, and so my mind constructed terrible dream escapes of disaster beyond my control, for which I could not be held responsible, and about which I felt terrible, and I would wake in a flood of relief that there was no war, no fire, no earthquake: a relief that I was safe, though I was not safe.

*

The moment that the woman inside her gate said, 'I let my husband decide,' I recognised it. I was out canvassing with the writer Mike Parker, a friend who'd been selected as Plaid Cymru's Westminster candidate for Ceredigion; we were going door to door, and they'd seen us coming, this couple, who were standing in their driveway. When Mike had greeted them both, it was the man who'd answered. She was some ten years older than me. I never learned her name, or what work she did, or if she worked, but I wonder if she saw it in my face, the recognition of her fearfulness, when she deferred that way to her husband, the way I'd seen it, years before, in the face of a college tutor. I'd been in my mid-twenties then, attending evening classes at community college, and one Saturday we were late coming back from a field trip, and my agitation was growing beyond control at what I feared awaited me at home. The tutor, a kind man in his sixties, began to ask what I was afraid of, and then stopped himself – but I'd seen it, his recognition, and it punctured the membrane of privacy; it was the beginning of seeing my fear from outside, and it was the beginning of shame.

In the abstract I felt a kind of understanding for this woman behind her gate. I know precisely how the questions, 'Why don't you just leave? Why didn't you just leave?' are unanswerable, though the answers are clear, because I know how it works, that heavily overused term, gaslighting. Perhaps he holds you against the wall by your wrist. *Stop it, you're hurting me*, you might say. He is close to losing control; he is trying hard to control his rage, his frustration, his own hurt; he's trying hard to control you, too, without losing control of himself. *What happened*, he says. *How am I hurting you? I haven't done anything. What's wrong with you? This is your fault. You said you wanted to go: so go. Get lost. Get out of here. Go.* But he's holding you by the wrist against the wall. Nothing happens, but everything happens. All that could happen happens, too, and does not happen – because he is controlling you, and he is controlling the narrative not just of your relationship, but of your person, your psyche. He says *You're imagining it. What happened? I didn't hurt you.* And of course he's right. It hardly hurt. There's no mark on your wrist. You might press it later, feeling for the bruise, feeling for the evidence, the truth of what happened, which is that he took control of you physically, and he threatened you – but without one word, without any risk to himself. He threatened you, and then he established that it was your fault that he had threatened you, but the threat was in your imagination, because he did not hurt you, or say anything that was a threat.

I should have felt compassion for this frightened woman standing behind her gate, but I did not feel compassion – I felt rage, a rage that returns to me uncontrolled, corrosive, destroying my capacity for compassion, for grief, undermining my capacity for love.

And I find myself at times wanting to hold onto that anger. It sustains me, and relieves me of responsibility. With that rage, I can believe in the simple binaries by which we conveniently navigate, by which we categorise blame, responsibility and agency: all those mutually exclusive terms like victim/perpetrator; oppressor/oppressed; strong/weak; powerful/disempowered. To be angry because something outrageous has been done to you is a way of being helpless without acknowledging being weak, because your anger makes you feel strong, and camouflages your fear.

That rage, when I saw my own abjection reflected in someone else, came on me once, unexpected and inappropriate, at a funeral. It was my neighbour, Morwen, who had died. She was buried on a cold February day, when the gusting wind blew the elderly mourners off balance. There were two kites mewling overhead, and the wind pushed them sideways too. I thought she would have liked to be attended by kites. She used to feed the birds. She remembered when there had been otters in the river, and water voles on the bank. Her family had lived in my house during her childhood; she remembered how it had looked when the barn still stood, before the bridge was built. She lived just over the road, and whenever I was away, she'd keep an eye on things. My spare key sat for years in a cup on her mantelpiece, in case something happened while I was away. If a parcel was delivered while I was out at work she would watch for the lights to see when I returned, and bring it round. She told me once, gesturing to the wilderness, 'I like your wild garden,' and I'd laughed and said that that was a polite name for it.

After the funeral, I came into the fug of the chapel vestry where the long tables were laid for tea under fluorescent lights. Two women were still busily wiping the last cups and plates and setting them out. I sat beside the minister, whom I recognised from a Welsh class I'd attended years before, when I'd first moved to the village. The group had met once a week in Y Barcud, a pub two miles up the road, rehearsing the rote phrases of conversational Welsh classes that echoed awkwardly in village halls and pubs and vestries and further education college classrooms all over rural Wales: 'Noswaith dda' if it was an evening class, and the call and response of 'Shwd dach chi?' and 'Da iawn, diolch,' and, depending on the season, 'Mae'r tywydd yn braf' or 'Mae hi'n oer'. Like most of those informal conversational groups, it fizzled out after the numbers dropped to two.

At the end of our table, a woman took up position with a capacious stainless steel pot of tea. She poured each of us a cup of peat-coloured liquid, and offered a refill as soon as anyone had taken a gulp. She stood there serving, filling and passing back cups and saucers while we sat and ate bara brith and buttered scones and swilled dark tea. I recognised the woman serving at my table, though I couldn't place her. She was my age. Her face was empty, and she smiled blandly, as though she was hardly present. I sat there among the mourners, flushed with distressed rage at her. My rage wasn't at what it represented in itself, her standing at the table serving tea, but at servility, and at her being a willing party to it, being an active agent in her own submissive role. I thought of Sartre's description of the waiter, which I read when I was about sixteen, but this did not seem a bad faith performance of servility, so much as a whole way of being, the embrace of a servile identity. I looked at her blank, smiling face and hated her. She was at that moment the embodiment of the one-down, submissive woman I had been asked to be, that most women, in one way or another, are so often asked to be.

She acted as a trigger, and I dreamed that night that I was still living with the man I'd left twenty-five years before, that I was once again trapped as I used to be. It was a dream in which I wanted to have a room of my own. I had presented my reasons, and my plea, and I was waiting, hoping, for his permission so that I could move into my own room. I was afraid of his response, of the consequence of having asked: he was going to be angry, and judge me for wanting something that seemed to reject him. Next door there were dogs kept in an enclosed yard. The turf had been dug over, as though they were pigs rather than dogs. It was dirty, full of turds and detritus – an image of what I had been doing, evidently, uncovering what was foul and best left hidden.

When I woke, I remembered that I had a room of my own. I had a home of my own. I had a whole life of my own. I was not trapped, and I needed no man's permission for anything, and the old rage surged through me that I ever had.

You can divest yourself of the detritus of a finished relationship, ridding yourself of its objects – in the rubbish, in the fire, and, with greater contempt, in the recycling. You can dispose of it all: the possessions, and the story that those possessions no longer tell. But fear is a kind of detritus you can't so easily divest yourself of. It lingers, unseen, and then something triggers its return to consciousness – a nervous woman behind her gate, deferring to her husband for an opinion; a woman at a funeral tea, serving – reminding you of who you used to be, and who you know you still are: fearing judgement, fearing anger, fearing control, and full of shame at your weakness, and rage at yourself for having been weak, for still being weak.

But perhaps that woman in the vestry revelled in her role; perhaps it denoted status, importance; perhaps it lent a meaning and value to her life, to be supporting those in grief. I wonder, now, how the old story fits, whether the dream, instead of being a return, like the whiff of corruption, wasn't detritus at all. Perhaps it was telling me a different story: that I have a room of my own, and not because I asked permission but because I gave myself permission; that I acted; that I had agency after all, despite my fear, despite the long aftermath of that fear; that it is not fear but the choice to act despite fear that can determine my life.

*

None of this goes through my mind as I stand in the path looking at the polecat looking at me – no memories of a woman in the chapel vestry or behind a gate; no memories of California; no thoughts about the meaning of my dreams. You don't think about fear in the moment of fear. Sometimes it is only afterwards, thinking back, that you even recognise that what you felt was fear.

In this moment, looking at the polecat, nothing goes through my mind at all. He faces me, unafraid. He looks at me and apprehends me in his polecat cognition, assesses how I smell and how I sound, and finds me uninteresting after all; he's more interested in getting it on with his girl.

Anything I think about this encounter is projection, as my response to those women was projection. Of course I will commit that heinous crime, anthropomorphism, if I attribute anything to him at all beyond acknowledging his existence, observing his appearance and what he does. But that is to objectify him; to reduce him to a thing, not a living creature to whom I respond in all the flawed and inadequate ways that I have learned to respond. I know that this is a polecat interrupted by me in the act or anticipation of mating; I can *know* nothing beyond that, perhaps. But there is still my experience of him. He looks at me without fear, and I experience his gaze as the gaze of an equal. I do not feel recognised or reacted to, or identified: I am, simply, observed.

My response is nothing like my familiar fear: it isn't fear of how he sees me, or what he might do; it isn't fear of danger, and it certainly isn't an annihilation of self in the face of wildness. It makes me for an instant pricklingly alive, because he looks at me in a way that upends the relationship of threat and fear, of power and weakness, of dominance and submission – before he turns away, and slips down the bank in pursuit of what I have so rudely interrupted.

12. Gannets

At the top of Indian Rock, with its view over the Bay towards San Francisco and the Golden Gate Bridge, which showed its red tower-tops in the fog, we returned to our shared and troubled past. Two young men were bouldering below us under an overhang, swearing each time they had to drop back off the rock, polished as marble. The steps cut out to the top were also polished smooth, all the surfaces slippery. There was no running water there where we could throw our sins in the Jewish tradition of atonement, but the effect was the same: a truth and reconciliation process; a letting go, and the beginning of deep friendship.

Down below us lay the network of freeways and railways whose traffic had marked my every waking and sleeping hour when I lived there. I used to stand on the station platform, waiting for a BART train to San Francisco, watching a red-tailed hawk circling, or American robins drunk on pyracantha berries, noticing how rarely, occasionally, someone would look to see what I was looking at, and frown, and look back at their newspaper, or book, or, later, their phone. Years after, watching people on the promenade in Aberystwyth from an upstairs café window, I remarked that no one looked up, and the man I was sitting with said he always looked up, a reflex to check for snipers. I thought at the time, caught in a new romance of discovery, that this was tragic war-zone drama, though later, when the gloss had worn off, I dismissed it as absurd self-importance.

How often I fell for men caught in their own pathologies. I was smitten so easily by a man's story of trauma or injury or despair. I didn't have any scars or really any stories worth telling, I thought – and I seemed always open to letting the urgency of their needs erase my own. It reminded me, thinking back, of the way in which a chemical element in a nutritious food – oxalic acid in spinach, say – can hinder the absorption of an essential nutrient; or the way in which lead poisoning works in the body over a long gradual period of exposure, slowing your responses, leaving you anaemic, weak, tired, and cognitively compromised.

Our accounting of the past at the top of Indian Rock did not involve forgiveness or the asking for forgiveness – that would have seemed like the perpetuation of a power relationship, a reinforcement of victim/perpetrator. Instead it entailed each of us hearing and being heard, apologising and accepting apology. Perhaps it was possible because with time, and distance, I had ceased at last to be afraid of him. Perhaps it was possible because I changed my relationship to fear.

Living in a state of fear leaves a permanent mark. You can't entirely unlearn it. But you can change what you do about it – fear, after all, does not tell the whole truth, either about danger, or about your capacity to deal with danger. Yet how compelling it is, charging through you when it happens, as if you've learned nothing. And even as it causes its familiar chemical damage, how alive it can make you feel, the common or garden fear that so many people share: fear of men, fear of violence, fear of being controlled, fear of heights.

The Castlemartin firing range at Range West, on the Pembrokeshire coast, is off limits to the general public. The British Mountaineering Council describes climbing here as 'truly unique' because of all the unexploded ordnance that you must avoid, which adds a different kind of risk to the appeal (or otherwise) of 'loose rock, abseil approaches, nesting birds and particularly fast incoming tides'. You have to attend a special training talk with the Ministry of Defence and register your details if you want to walk or climb here – it gives you access during gaps in the live firing.

On a shelf of rock high above the sea, the terror takes me. It always does at some point when I go climbing. I'm belaying my partner, Tony, who has climbed out of sight, and out of hearing, up to the clifftop. I know, as a kind of hypothetical fact which has no meaning, that when he's reached the top he will secure himself, will give two tugs on the rope to let me know it's safe for me to follow him, and that he'll have me securely on the rope as I climb. I know that once I begin to climb, the worst that can happen is that I might slip a few inches and scrape my knees – that he, and the rope, and my harness, will hold me.

But these are merely so-called facts. My fear has got away from my control and I am thinking bad thoughts about falling, bouncing against the cliff, down into the sea – or, not so much thinking, as gibbering inside *what if what if....* What if he falls? What if he reaches the top and blacks out? (There's no reason he would black out, I tell myself; that's crazy thinking – but *what if... what if?*) What if I misinterpret his tugs on the rope, because the rope gets caught in a crack, and I climb too soon, before he's belayed himself? What if the tug on the rope never comes?

There is no mobile signal, and there is no one within miles of us. Once we signed in and set off, climbing the gate that says 'NO ACCESS', we were really on our own: no other climbers or walkers were listed on the day's sign-in sheet. We abseiled down to this shelf where I'm sitting, so there is no getting out of it, either – no going back. The only way I can escape is by climbing, but I sit trembling with my back pressed to the crag, my thoughts racing, my heart racing.

The first time I went climbing, back in 2016, I thought I could overcome fear by facing it, but the fear of heights has never changed since stepping up to that little limestone crag in Mull. The terror takes me every time. It happened at Ynys Lochtyn, when I was three feet off the ground, and couldn't find a handhold without first pushing myself higher with a foot on a little lip – but couldn't step back down again, either, because that would have meant stepping into nothingness. And it happened on an arête at Shepherd's Crag in the Lake District; that's when I discovered for the first time what climbers meant by 'exposure'. Following Tony up that arête, which began under tree cover, I came out above the treeline, and suddenly, everything to my left and right and below me was gone. I was hardly aware of the tension on the rope tautly held above me. The fact that I was safe, that though I might slip I would fall less than a foot, was meaningless; it did not even register as noise – it had abandoned me, that knowledge. Instead I was pressed against a sharp spine of rock, my right arm trembling as I groped frantically for a handhold. I thought I might never move again. My bowels didn't turn to water – that happens in the anticipation of climbing. Instead of the fight or flight response of jettisoning ballast, it was as though my body's routine functions had shut down. Even to breathe felt almost unnatural. I didn't feel pain: I felt the weakness of my arm, the trembling in my leg, which I registered as a distant problem of the future, and I felt an enormous pressure on my lungs. Something was compressing my chest so that I couldn't breathe. There is not any choice, once you've begun: you're committed, because to climb down is no different than to climb up – it's worse, in fact, because you have to look down. I knew I had to get control of my mind, my bad thoughts that threatened to get away into disaster and impossibility. It was not control of my shaking arm I needed, but control of my shaking consciousness. Breathe, I said, trying to breathe.

Breathe. Breathe *out*. Again. It felt as muscular and deliberate as lifting a great weight. Slowly, my mind stilled. And then at last I could express the terror that I was not feeling so immediately. A whisper first, and then louder. I swore at Tony above me, out of sight. I swore at the rope, at the rock, at the rain that was beginning to fall, at the void that I turned my mind away from with a kind of deliberateness that was also as muscular a process as the effort to breathe had been a moment before. I had to choose not to think about the empty space around me and behind me and below me; I had to think in the narrowest terms, so narrow that it was not thought, to shut down my imagination, which had gone into an erratic hyperdrive. The saying 'letting your imagination run away with you' might mean imagining things that aren't true, but there my imagination ran away with me into things that seemed only too true: danger, for one; the extreme likelihood of pain. But I was not in danger. There was a man above me, with a belay device on the rope that would lock it in place and make it impossible to slip. He himself was securely anchored; he too could not slide. The rope was so firmly tied in to the harness that was tight around my legs and midriff that there was danger, only, of skinning my palms and wrists and elbows, banging my knees. I knew I was not going to fall, and yet my imagination ran away from me into what was real but untrue: the certainty that I was going to fall.

I concentrated on breathing until it became no longer a conscious choice to breathe in or out, but a natural process. And then my mind was narrowed only to the feel and look of the rock before me and above me: its slick surface, smoothed by wind, water, and the hands and feet of all the other people who had climbed there and not died. I had to look down for footholds, but I controlled what I saw: I shut the doors of my peripheral vision, and I shut out everything below what I was looking for – a protuberance or little ledge, or a crack into which I could lodge my foot. And when at last I placed my foot there and launched my weight upwards, scrabbling with one outstretched hand for a hold that might or might not be there, there was no thought but the necessity of movement, of action. Everything in my overactive imagination shouted at me that this was precisely what I should not do, but I shut it down. And as I scrabbled, my fingers and palm closed over a lip of rock that I could grasp fully and there was a euphoric sensation of release, a kind of joyful delirium, as above me Tony said *there's a nice juggy hold...* and I swore at him that I had it, swore at him because I could, because it was safe to, because I had taken the risk.

Holding onto that solid rocky protrusion, I was full of the returning knowledge that above me there would be others, too, that I would be able to climb to safety.

But here at Range West, I am not even climbing yet. I am sitting, feeding out rope as my partner climbs somewhere out of sight above me. My heart is galloping. My thoughts are not thoughts but a dark shapeless thrashing.

It's a beautiful place to be. The rock is warm in the sunlight; birds pass out at sea – silent fulmars, occasionally, on their stiff wing blades; gulls I can't identify. But I don't see any of that.

There are the two tugs on the rope: he's reached the top, he's safe, he's conscious, he's secured himself, none of my bad thoughts have come to pass, but *what if....* Now I have to undo what's anchoring me to the rock, remove the cams and nuts, and clip the carabiners onto a loop on my harness, out of the way, and then give him the signal, my own tug on the rope, to tell him I'm ready to climb and that he should take in the slack. But I can't move. My hands are cold, sweating, cramped. *What if... what if* – what if I'm not tied in properly? What if I slip? What if my harness gives way.... Whimpering, I lean my head back against the warm slab of rock that I need to climb. I know he's waiting, wondering, starting to get worried because I've given him no signal. The pressure to move builds; I know I have to act but I can't act; I can't even look at the rock: it would mean seeing that I am on a ledge high above the sea.

Then, a few feet away, a gannet coasts by, at eye level, shining in the sun. I latch onto it. I follow it, and beyond it is the sea, the distant straight horizon. Then the gannet turns and comes back and passes me again, wings flat and straight. I've never seen a gannet this close before: I can see all the detail of its yellow head, its strange pale blue eye checking me.

A gannet caught in sunlight, out over the sea, shining like a great white black-tipped cross, like that bird appearing from the fog in *The Voyage of the Dawn Treader* – that is about as close to my understanding of holy as I could ever get. 'Spiritual', some might say; perhaps it's what spiritual means to people who use that word, or maybe it's something akin to what New Age followers might call a spirit animal.

But if there is such a thing as a spirit animal – either that of Western neoshamanist belief, or of the cultures from which the idea has been taken – I don't suppose that it's one you get to choose. Surely a spirit animal would have something to tell you about yourself, like the unexpected absurd penguin in *Fight Club*. But none of the qualities I associate with gannets (grace, elegance, power, speed, a propensity for breaking their necks on impact with the water) are qualities that could in any way be associated with this particularly short, clumsy, fearful, thick-ankled, sweating klutz that my spirit, if I have one, calls home. Then again, a gannet is a stinking great bird with a sword for a beak, and ridiculous webbed feet.

I never see gannets when I hope to see them, when I look for them, but when I do see them out to sea they seem to be a portent, to have some message for me (in fact they are a portent: if they're diving off Cardigan Bay it usually means porpoises are around, or will be soon).

Of course, gannets have no message for me, so I might as well just get on with what I have to do, the way this gannet is getting on with what it has to do, which is a whole lot more significant (fish, survival, perpetuation of the species) than my puny effort, secure on this shelf of rock, to grapple with fear.

Trembling, I undo the anchor, clip the gear onto my harness, double check the figure-of-eight knot. I tug on the rope, and watch the slack sliding up the rock as somewhere above me Tony is taking it in. He feels the resistance of my body's weight, and stops. The rope dangles, swaying slightly, disappearing beyond a slight overhang. I rub my hands together, breathe out, shut down my mind, and then I'm climbing. Once I start, the fear turns into pure adrenaline. It's acute, sharp – my mind is stripped of noise and thought and process, conscious only of the unfolding moment. And there's no denying it: the only time I felt this alive, this centred, this immediate, was when, decades ago, a man took me and threw me against a wall, grabbed me, pushed me out onto the landing and there, to my left, the void of the long flight of stairs gaped below me.

'There was a gannet,' I gabble, when I reach the clifftop. 'A gannet....' Tony is smiling at me as I lie down on the flat rabbit-bitten grass away from the edge, vaguely trying to untie myself from the rope's end. He's seen me like this so many times: euphoric and giddy with the endorphin rush of overcoming fear.

13. Risk Assessment

In the autumn, the mobile mammography unit appears again in Morrison's car park, not far from the River Rheidol. For long weeks as the year turns, and the flood risk begins again to rise, it slouches there like a white threatening reminder.

The year that I turned fifty, my annual letter from Breast Test Wales contained no invitation to go to Swansea for a mammogram. Instead it told me that my risk was now statistically the same as that of other women my age, and I would no longer have a yearly test. I would not be making the journey south in the autumn, watching the magpies, waiting for the beech veneer door to open. Instead, every three years I would be invited to attend this long white mobile unit in the supermarket car park in Aberystwyth for a reading of the signs.

Sooner or later, over a three-year period, most of the women above fifty who I know or see in this town and its hinterland of villages and farms will drive here, or get off the bus by the petrol station, and steel themselves before mounting the steps to the door, with their appointment letter tucked in a bag or clutched in their hand. All of us will wait the two or three weeks for a result, watching the season change, their risk the same as my risk, their fear the same as mine.

Most of the time, it's hard to remember that this car park where the unit is stationed, and all these low-lying levels, are in the flood plain of the Rheidol. Usually, the river slips along silently by the playing fields where the air ambulance lands, then under the road, behind the supermarket and its rubbish bins, where the kites now prospect. It meets its twin, the Ystwyth, behind the marina where the glossy boats are berthed, the ghosts of the busy boatbuilding town that Aberystwyth used to be, when water was a road, an opportunity, not a barrier or a threat.

Both rivers broke their banks in the storms of January 2014. The Rheidol flooded the playing fields, the new redbrick housing estate, the supermarket and its car park. At the sea's edge, high tides and a storm surge tore up the promenade, scattering coping stones and paving slabs, iron railings and iron benches. The morning after the storm there was no longer any promenade raised above the sea: the shore had moved inland, leaving the pelican crossing and 30mph speed-limit signs sticking up out of three feet of sand by the evacuated seafront hotels, whose basements and cellars had filled with kelp and crabs and seawater. That morning, people walked silently in ones and twos on the shore that had been a road, moving slowly as though stunned, dazed by the damage, and the force that had caused the damage.

Sooner or later, water will no doubt reclaim all this lowland. The Iron Age hill fort of Pen Dinas will be an island, and the war memorial's bare-breasted figure of Humanity below the town castle will lean out at the end of what will be a promontory again, her copper feet lapped by the sea. Inland, where I live at an elevation of 700 feet, the uplands will rise above marshland; the air will be full of the noise of waterbirds, if there are any left, and further up the coast, if someone is still around to look out from the ramparts of Harlech Castle, they will hear water washing at the walls far below, as it did centuries ago when Bendigeidfran looked out to sea and saw the Irish king's ships approaching. Starlings, ravens, eagles and salmon then were the carriers of wisdom; what will these species carry into the flooded future?

*

Back in 2020, for weeks on end, my older daughter could not go outside. Nor could she talk much, on the phone – my evening, her midday – because her throat hurt. Beyond her home, the sky was dark orange; one morning it turned red and day never came. She was some distance from the nearest fires, five of them, but they were all around: to the north, the northeast, and east and southeast, and, for a few days, when Point Reyes burned, to the west. California's fire season that year was the worst in its recorded history, in sheer volume – worse than two years earlier, when the town of Paradise had burnt down.

The last time I'd been back to California, in 2019 for her wedding, we'd driven through burn zones of the previous year's fires. The rebuilding, everywhere, was rapid, massive. That trite political slogan, after the worst of the pandemic, *build back better*, might have had some weight in California then, but the Californian way always seemed to be *build back bigger*.

There were probably fires somewhere in the state most years that I lived in California, but I don't think I would have paid much attention to them. The northern California landscape, with its manzanita and redwoods, is in part made of fire: some tree species rely on fire to germinate. They weren't such devastating fires then, or not for northern California's human inhabitants; they rarely threatened major population centres, or their edges. The exception was the Oakland hills firestorm of 1991, which destroyed some 2,800 homes in the East Bay. My daughter was three years old at the time; we lived across the bay in San Francisco. I recall the sky turning orange, the smell of ash. The smoke plume went seven miles out over the Pacific, and that seemed remarkable then (in 2020, the smoke plume reached the east coast and then crossed the Atlantic to Europe). We moved to a house at the edge of the burn zone in Oakland the following year. Half a block from where we lived (in a timber house surrounded by dry eucalyptus), cracked concrete foundations and floors marked out the footprint of the burned houses, and the only vertical structures that remained were the dented, earthquake-braced water heaters which dotted the hillside. The owners were waiting for rebuild permissions or contractors. They had marked their loss and their intention to return with little altars and temporary potted gardens. And they did return: the building site was huge, loud. They, too, built back bigger, as though through bulk and mass they hoped to undo their loss, and repudiate the threat of its recurrence.

The East Bay firestorm occurred two years almost to the day after the Loma Prieta earthquake of 1989. When I moved to San Francisco, three weeks after that earthquake, the aftershocks had ceased, but the destruction was visible for months: the detritus fallen from damaged buildings; the row of houses a few blocks away from where I lived, walls cracked and not yet inspected, cordoned off with police tape; the empty Embarcadero freeway, which was afterwards pulled down; the collapsed Nimitz freeway, which was destroyed and rebuilt elsewhere; the collapsed section of the Bay Bridge – and the Marina neighbourhood, where a fire had burned out of control for three days, built on landfill that suffered liquefaction. The term *liquefaction* haunted me, the notion that solid ground could behave like liquid. From the beginning, I felt the very ground I walked on in California was unsafe.

Back then, earthquake was the perennial, perpetual risk, and fire was exceptional, a risk during the driest months, before rainfall in November. Now the rainfall comes later or barely at all; in recent years, the fire season hardly ends.

In 2021, my daughter bought a place four hours north of the San Francisco Bay Area – a house on an off-grid, two-and-a-half-acre lot in the Shasta-Trinity National Forest. There's a high fire risk, but fire isn't a particular source of anxiety for her. 'Where isn't there a threat, now?' she says. 'Where is safe, or will stay safe?' She hates the thought of flooding, and of hurricanes. She went to college on the east coast and remembers the sky turning green in a tornado. It terrified her. But fire? Fire, she says, is part of that landscape. She feels it belongs there as much as she does, and loving the land means living with fire. 'You have to accept that your house might burn down,' she says. 'You hope it won't, but if it does, you rebuild.' If it were to happen, she'd rebuild in cob, not timber.

Perhaps even five years ago it might have seemed a risky move – although, given earthquakes, to live in California at all can seem a dangerous choice. But now, wherever you live, the very notion of feeling safe, of believing your home can be an impregnable fortress, an impenetrable shelter from the elements, seems delusional.

The stone bwthyn where I live was flooded in 2008, and for years afterwards, I wanted to move to a hilltop. Every time it rained hard, I walked from window to window like a caged cat, checking the weather, listening for the rising river.

Water itself isn't exactly what I fear where my house is concerned; it is what the water brings with it, and what the water leaves behind. No image of the aftermath of flooding conveys its stench. When the road floods, after heavy sustained rain, all the desiccated roadkill that the kites and corvids haven't taken, flattened into the pitted tarmac, comes loose and washes away with the dog shit, the litter, the manure dropped from the passing muck spreader or splashed by the dairy herd moved from one field to the next. There's chicken manure transported from the poultry units, sheep dung off the fields, fertiliser, silage, leaked diesel and petrol and oil – and sewage. In a built-up area, you might have to deal with other people's sewage, and your own, backing up through the pipes, but in a rural area, it's breached septic tanks.

When my house was flooded, the water did little damage, except to six inches of plaster. It came in under the doors, and departed through the porous walls. But it deposited a thick layer of stinking muck over everything. Even now, when the field drain gets blocked and the stream comes down the exposed rock by the house and spreads into a lake over the septic tank before draining into the river, it's that muck that I dread. *Get in touch with nature*, we say, but floodwater brings you close to nature in forms that you want no contact with at all: faeces, protazoa, decomposing bodies, and what they in turn carry.

I have my defences now, front and back, my little levees. My house is below road level, and I've taken other action, too, digging out decades or maybe even a century of accumulated muck in front, to uncover an old cobbled pavement a foot below the level of the doorstep. It slopes away from the building in an old drainage strategy that works for now. Perhaps over the decades the levees will rise and rise, and my house will slowly descend into darkness.

When the volume of rain is too much for the field drains, and the stream rushes down by the house instead, a rime of detritus shows the path of the receding water: a tangle of moss, twigs, sheep's wool, pink or orange twine, black rags of baling plastic. And washed up along the line of muck, the soil and sheep dung and stones, there's always a scatter of drowned rodents – shrews, or wood mice, their tiny bodies bloated.

As it warms again after a storm, if it's a flash flood in summer, the stench rises with the steam off the waterlogged land. And days, sometimes weeks later, when it's wet again, and warm, the smell of that decomposing detritus returns.

Flooding leaves invisible detritus, too. Every time it rains hard, I am agitated, alert to a danger that is real and possible, as I imagine anyone feels who is at risk of flooding, or has been flooded in the past. I take precautions, but know they might not be enough. I keep empty sandbags, now, and a bin of sand, against those times when the council's highways department will be too late because of more urgent emergencies. I read the weather warnings of heavy rain and possible flooding and I plan accordingly, clearing the sump, ensuring I'll be home. When the rain comes, particularly after a long dry spell which leaves the ground hard, so that everything runs off, I put on my boots and go up the road to clear the drains. If it's really sustained, and the road and field drains are overwhelmed, the garden beginning to turn into a lake, eventually I move everything vulnerable off the downstairs floors and place them on the chairs, the table, or take them upstairs: plug strips, floor lamps, rugs, shoes. Then I go to bed, and lie awake and listen to the rain on the roof, the splash of passing cars, the river, rising.

Perhaps now, with our perception of the world changed, nearly everyone shares something of the sense of existential unsafety left by flood and by fire. Nothing that we do to try to slow climate change and species extinction, to try to prevent the world becoming, by our own doing, inhospitable to humans, will make it safe for us. Our little acts of ethical consumption, which provide comfort for a short while because we're doing the right thing, might let us believe that if only everyone else acted this way, we would not need to be afraid. But none of those minor changes – an electric car, or carbon offsetting; planting trees or going vegan – can tell us how to live with the ever-present existential experience of unsafety. Then again, why should the world feel safe or be safe for us? Perhaps our newly discovered collective anxiety is not so damaging as we might at first think. Perhaps, on the contrary, it is a more natural state than the comfortable unconscious feeling of safety that so many of us have lost. Maybe it's a necessary corrective, after a short evolutionary blip, to acknowledge and learn to live with our own vulnerability, individually and collectively, like any other species.

Up on the common, the derelict farmhouse has been sold, along with thirty-five acres of land. It went for £250,000; the building will need to be pulled down and rebuilt. Unscheduled viewings were permitted, but the upstairs was inaccessible: the stairs were unsafe. The thirty-five acres includes the boggy land where the curlews nest. This spring, as I walked up out of the village to the common, John stopped beside me in his ancient Land Rover to ask if I'd heard any yet – but I'd only heard one, briefly, in the distance. 'Pum pâr, flynydde nôl,' he said, holding his five fingers spread for emphasis. I can't imagine there'd still be five pairs: recently there has been news every year of curlews declining precipitously, particularly in Wales. Years ago, when I first moved here, and John saw me carrying binoculars, he stopped and asked what I'd seen, and I learned the Welsh name for redstart and swallow and kestrel. He's one of the few older neighbours who doesn't switch to English out of misplaced politeness if I hesitate and search for a word, or ask him to repeat what he's said. He lets me carry on, so that I don't get hung up on what I don't know, but rely instead upon what I do. I suppose it's largely the same with any form of learning. At some point with a language, as with birds, you acquire that capacity for instant recognition and exclusion, even if you are dogged occasionally by the superficially similar meadow and rock pipits of Welsh: rhyw versus rhew, say – sex and ice.

Fifteen years ago, I used to hear the curlews from the village, but now I never do. Late in the spring, I heard at least three calling, so they were still holding on somehow. What will happen up there now that the land has been sold? Perhaps whoever's bought it will drain the bog and try to turn it into pasture –

but perhaps not: perhaps someone has bought that land to preserve it. Whether it's rewilded with trees, or turned into productive pasture, or built over with chicken sheds, that will be the end for the curlews.

Loss is what I tend to focus on, in gloomy prognostication, but change isn't only loss. There are gains, too. At midnight I go out, the first night of autumn. The street light is still on but the bats that zip back and forth at dusk over the pond have gone elsewhere, along with the insects. The river is low; for ten days it's been overcast, sullen, as though promising rain. But the rain hasn't come. There are small trout above the bridge – six inches at most, but a good dozen of them. Despite the new poultry units upstream, which felt like a doom on the river, the water quality seems, so far, to be unaffected.

I listen to the night sounds. Eurig's great shining wind turbine above the village is quiet for once, turning slowly in a slight breeze from the southwest. When it's from the east there's a high continual whine and the *whump-whump-whump* of its blades. Sometimes if the wind is due west, I hear the thump of the eleven turbines up on Mynydd Bach.

Tonight there's hardly any wind. Saturn is low, a warm yellow to the southeast; there's the small rustle of a vole or a shrew, perhaps even a large beetle trundling through dry weeding detritus that I've left in a heap. Further off, I can hear the river slipping over the shale under the bridge, where the course widens.

But now something large is in the water, interrupting the flow, not so much splashing as churning. I think it's just some temporary disruption that's happened elsewhere and the water disturbance has come downstream – a cow blundering into the river, maybe, changing the volume and sound here, by the bridge. But the sound continues, and then alters, and moves upstream. A car approaching along the main road eliminates other noise, but in the silence after it has passed, there's that same churn of water, moving against the current, towards the wood. Only one thing could make that sound against the current: it must be an otter.

Once, not long after I moved here, I found otter spraint when everywhere was flooded and a stream was running down from the field. There's been no other sign in twenty years of living here, but tonight, it seems, something has been gained: an otter has come upriver to visit. Perhaps he will stick around now and become a new neighbour.

By the road to Swyddffynnon, there's a flock of starlings bickering with each other in a field bounded by gorse hedges. When I see them in their large winter gatherings like this, I find it difficult to conceive of how their numbers are dropping rapidly, to imagine that extinction of such a common bird could be possible.

Starlings squabble all the time, in a grating, noisy conflict. These ones roost nearby, in the winter, in a bit of forestry, and sometimes before heading for sleep they make a compelling black murmuration against the red sky and silhouetted wind turbines of Mynydd Bach. Now, working their way across the field in search of food, they are all glossy bustling bossiness, and they seem unafraid, except when they are at the back of the flock. At first the continual squabbling seems to be random conflict, as, a few at a time, they take off and land. But then a pattern begins to emerge: there's nothing random about it. They are working a field the way they work a murmuration, each with close attention to the birds immediately around them, so that the whole flock seems to participate in an immense collective choreography. I suppose that the birds at the front have best pickings for a short while, though they also carry the risk of attack; the birds in the middle have the best protection against an assault by a sparrowhawk, but have to work harder for food; and the birds at the back are vulnerable, exposed, and with the slimmest pickings – and it is they who, after a short while, reach an intolerable level of unease (or resentment, or hunger), and take flight, a few at a time, to the front of the flock, exposing a new group, now at the back of the flock, to danger. There is a continual cycle as a cluster of birds at the back flies to the front; the birds at the front object, and there are scuffles, but that settles down until the birds newly exposed at the back in turn take flight to the front, and repeat the cycle again.

Watching them, voyeur, from behind the hedge, I almost miss the sparrowhawk skimming low along the road ahead of me, until she shoots up and over the gorse at the starlings. The whole lot rise as one, and she is startled, confused, loses the grace and speed of her attack, checks her pursuit, and lumbers into the hedge, where she sits hunched up, as if embarrassed.

I suppose I could view the starlings' behaviour as a tidy metaphor for sharing resources and shared vulnerability, but instead, watching them, I see only an existential threat so pervasive, so continual, that it is a fundamental state of being. And I wonder about the experience of unsafety in which women usually live without being fully aware, something that's set in motion from the moment of birth, when adults begin to shape their care of us according to our biological sex. Unlike birds we take precautions; we assess relative risk; we perform our compulsive rituals against it happening (*touch wood, fingers crossed, god forbid, inshallah, baruch hashem*), and we act despite perceived risk. Still, it's so pervasive that we hardly recognise it, that state of being primed against existential threat, until it's brought into focus by a particular incident, private or public.

Maybe that is what most humans have begun again to feel. The awareness of wild forces beyond our control, of a future of flood and fire and famine, perhaps now in one sense makes all of us, whatever our gender, experience something like agoraphobia. I don't mean agoraphobia in the common use of the term, to be afraid of open spaces, but the formal definition of the term, which is to be afraid, as the NHS puts it rather ungrammatically, 'of being in situations where escape might be difficult or that help wouldn't be available if things go wrong.'

Of course, like all pop psychology, it's nonsense to suggest we are all agoraphobic as a result of climate change and mass species extinction. It's worse than nonsense: easy pop psychology reduces and generalises what is complex and particular; it finds a satisfying label for a list of symptoms, and is gratifying because it makes intuitive sense out of what is opaque.

And to suggest that we might all be suffering a form of agoraphobia diminishes the actual lived experience of those who are diagnosed with this or with other phobias, who experience a seriously reduced quality of life, who are pathologised by individuals and social institutions.

Nevertheless, perhaps agoraphobia (and how people deal with it – perhaps all so-called pathological fear and ways of managing it) has something useful to tell us about adapting to an inescapable present and future that feels existentially unsafe.

One difference, experientially, between fear and phobia is a quality of certainty and inevitability. Whether fear is sudden or continual, it has peaks and troughs, and it might be resolved; what is feared isn't inevitable. By contrast, phobia has a quality of certainty and dread (for me at least – about wasps, for example). It constitutes a state of being quite distinct from the changeable feeling of fear.

With phobia, you calculate risk in ways that diverge wildly from the mathematical calculation of probability. With phobia, to consider the mathematical probability of an event that you fear is like looking at the strange schematics of a medieval map: you wouldn't know how to navigate by it; it would lead you out of the known world into danger (*here be dragons*). For me, to consider acting on the notion that wasps don't sting unless they're disturbed would be dangerous and nonsensical, because wasps are constitutionally a threat. The only way to reduce risk is to avoid them, but you can't avoid them.

According to phobic probability, the likelihood of a feared event increases towards imminent certainty the more time that elapses without it occurring. You can't ward it off, no matter what precautions you take: it is inevitable. This might seem like a defence or survival mechanism that's triggered when to all appearances it's unnecessary, one that becomes inefficient or chronic and causes more harm than help. But perhaps what seems to be a damaging maladaptation might now have advantages. Like any fear, phobia in its most extreme forms limits what you may do, but despite the state of existential unsafety it leaves you in, you have to carry on, with something like a radical optimism of the will.

Our fear, now, of risk, of the certainty of disaster no matter what we do, might not seem phobic – but perhaps that's only because it is a shared fear, a shared understanding of risk. That shared sense is that the risk is existential and inevitable, like phobic fear: it's a state of unsafety, and yet, despite what is inevitable, we have to carry on with a kind of willed optimism, hoping for reprieve.

Beyond the gorse hedge where the sparrowhawk has landed, the starlings are wheeling in formation. They sweep over the far hedge and back, and then they come down again in the field. The sparrowhawk cannot make an unseen approach: she has lost her advantage, and they know it. The evidence of the threat remains, but for now the starlings' assessment of imminent risk has changed. The worst will happen, but it has not yet happened, and in their temporary reprieve, they resume their squabbling progression across the mossy grass.

14. An Unkindness to Birdwatchers

At sunset, a flock of jackdaws swoop and clatter about beyond the third-floor window of the hospital's cardiac ward. To the southeast there's a view of the National Library on the hill, its pale stone illuminated by the setting sun, and to the southwest the Iron Age hill fort of Pen Dinas is silhouetted against the sky. My home lies ten long miles away, somewhere beyond the National Library, the hills, the Rheidol and the Ystwyth, and the Iron Age hill fort of Gaer Fawr, but I can't go home. 'Oh, the starlings!' exclaims one of my fellow patients, as the jackdaws stream past the window in the fading light. I try and fail to suppress it, my incredulity that she could mistake jackdaws for starlings. How could anyone who spends time in Aberystwyth in the winter not be able to recognise what is or is not a flock of starlings?

It's October, when the starlings are just beginning to gather, but by January the roost reaches its winter peak, and the murmuration over the pier, numbering in the tens of thousands, brings people to the town from miles away. It brings other birds, too. A peregrine and a sparrowhawk often attend, and in 2021, night-time footage from a BBC Winter Watch camera under the pier revealed a barn owl taking a sleeping bird.

Near sunset, the starlings converge from the north, the east and the south, in small groups and large, joining together to wheel over the Old College and the sea front, spattering everyone as they pass on their way to the main gathering. It's one of the great moments of coordination when two groups join together and there are no crashes, no faltering. Each day in the hour before sundown, the promenade is lined with people of all ages, some sitting in the shelters with their chips and ketchup, some with cameras set up on tripods, those in the know prepared with umbrellas or hoods or hats – and a few out at sea in kayaks. Maybe a hundred people waiting, watching. It's a wild spectacle without human intervention. There are no interpretation boards or signs, no mediation of ownership, no rules, screens or barriers. Nearby, down at the tideline, ignored or unnoticed, the little orange-legged turnstones chase the waves out and scurry from the water as it returns.

I know it doesn't matter that this woman in the next bed can't distinguish a jackdaw from a starling, and I try to stop myself from pointing out her mistake. I feel all the force of that well-known *xkcd* comic strip, 'Duty Calls', in which a figure seated at a computer is asked by a person from the next room, 'Are you coming to bed?' and they reply, 'I can't. This is important.... Someone is *wrong* on the internet.' The woman next to me hasn't asked, so why correct her? Why the urge to tell her she's wrong? The mistake doesn't make any difference in the world; it has no consequences, but there's a compulsion to point it out, to show that I know more than she knows. Is this what it feels like, the mansplaining compulsion: the urgent need to tell, to explain, to correct, no matter the context, the relationship? I recall my correction about American crows, but I can't keep myself from doing it. I can't resist. And when I've said to her, 'Actually, they're jackdaws,' I recognise the look on her face – slightly bemused, a little irritated, a withdrawal from me.

There are many things she could know about my interests and activities that I am not embarrassed by, things I would not hide or deny or downplay, but instead, birdsplaining like that, I've outed myself as a *twitcher*. I see it in her expression: the pity and mild contempt.

*

It's easy to see why the term *twitcher* is used derisively by non-birdwatchers. Those interested in birds – or the embarrassing ones, at least – are twitchy with obsessive focus; some are socially awkward, and the obsession is laughable. Not me, though. Yes, I'm interested in birds, but of course I'm not like *that*. After all, I'm not one of them: I don't keep a life list; I don't even know how many bird species I have seen, and I don't go tearing off up the A487 to Anglesey for the great spotted cuckoo, or racing down the coast to St David's Head for a sight of the snowy owl, or rock up at an MP's garden in Pembrokeshire, joining the line of scope-wielding anoraks (OK, camouflage and Gore-Tex) intent on ticking the night heron that's taken up residence. Nor am I part of the group that pays its RSPB subs and goes for a little Sunday or summer amble along the gravelled flat pathways of the nearest reserve, to sit down in a hide and train my expensive binoculars or telescope on a bittern that's 'showing well' in the reed bed. I might like birds, and I might like looking at birds, but I find all of that behaviour laughable, something that other birdwatchers do. Who would want to be associated with such an embarrassing, geeky identity?

In popular culture, twitchers are depicted as obsessive, white, middle-aged, middle-class, socially challenged and physically unfit men with poor dress sense. They are fair game, socially speaking, and may still be mocked; they are in the same class as the trainspotter who stands vigil at the end of a station platform, clutching his wrinkled plastic Tesco bag and notebook (though it's more likely now to be a phone or camera).

A 2012 episode of *Midsomer Murders* goes all out with birdspotter caricatures, featuring a twitchers' murderous competition over 'ticking' a rare vagrant (a fictitious blue-crested hoopoe). The programme seemed designed to trigger birder outrage with its outlandish depiction of competitive interest, and ridiculous (though evidently knowing) birding mistakes. The perpetrator is a wild exaggeration of all the tropes: he's socially inept, wears abominable sandals and huge glasses, and around his neck hangs a pair of binoculars so massive that the weight should have pulled him into a horizontal stoop (Mark Cocker's description of attendees wearing their binoculars at the annual Bird Fair points to the painful accuracy of this particular ridicule). The other Midsomer twitchers aren't much better, their bird preoccupation taking absurd expression. In response, 'real' birders (which is to say birders on online birding forums), fell into the trap that had been laid for them: they objected vociferously to the 'laziness' of the researchers for getting all the bird details wrong ('it is shocking the writers couldn't do five minutes' research to find what birds would be seen in typical British countryside'), thereby validating exactly the stereotype that the programme mocked. Although some found the mistakes funny, they didn't seem to realise the joke was on them. 'All the usual TV clichés about birdwatchers,' complained one. 'Laughable but for the wrong reasons.' Another found it hilarious: 'Apart from the netted greenfinch and the fictitious "blue-crowned hoopoe", every bird mentioned was North American... forget the Scillies and Fair Isle, clearly Midsomer is the place to go birding!' Others didn't find any humour in it at all: 'Not the first time Midsomer has got bird-related stuff miles wrong,' grumbled one disaffected viewer.

I acknowledge that I share it, the popular culture contempt for birdwatchers, even if I too shudder at television drama mistakes – the sound of swifts in a frozen February landscape, say, or the sound of a kite to represent the call of a circling buzzard. I have a violent disinclination to being in any way associated with well-known – if stereotyped – birdwatcher characteristics and behaviours. The respected expertise of high-profile TV presenters aside, it's a social liability to be seen as a twitcher, that caustic designation by non-birdwatchers which collapses any difference between passing interest and abject obsession.

I know my views of birdwatchers are dated, formed in the 1970s, and reinforced the way all stereotypes are reinforced, by noting the examples that affirm rather than challenge my preconceptions, but it's illuminating to see that process in action in others. When the results of a study on boredom were reported in 2022, birdwatching featured very prominently. 'World's "most boring" people revealed', announced *The Week*, and declared: 'Birdwatchers are perceived to be the most boring people, according to a new study called *Boring People: Stereotype Characteristics, Interpersonal Attributions, and Social Reactions*.' *The Week* illustrated this with a photograph of a birdwatcher looking through binoculars (though broke the stereotype by depicting a woman). Meanwhile an *Observer* headline claimed: 'Birdwatchers, church-goers and TV addicts are considered dull, according to new research', while the article below it declared that: 'A new study has supposedly pinpointed the most boring people alive: birdwatchers, accountants, data analysts and everyone who works in insurance.'

However, the study itself does not anywhere mention birdwatching. Instead it is 'animal observation' that is one of the top hobbies identified by participants as boring, and this is qualified within the tables of data with the subset of exemplars, 'bird watching; ant study'. The study's authors themselves note carefully that they 'set out to examine the *stereotype* that people hold about boring people, not the actual individual characteristics that boring people possess' – and the reporting seems to have illustrated this rather well.

I'm guilty of giving a warm and welcoming home to all this prejudice because it's not only in *Midsomer* and online discussion forums that birdwatchers live up to the stereotypes: in my experience, they often do so IRL, as it were. Part of what fuels my unease, and enables my prejudices to be reinforced rather than challenged, is the largely male exclusivity of this interest and its associated stereotypes. Most birdwatchers (birders, twitchers) are men, and most writing about birds – what I tend to think of as 'ornithography', a genre of nature writing all its own – is by men.

Some of that writing is moving and beautiful;

some of it is aggravating, but women are largely absent from almost all of it, including from such social histories as Stephen Moss' unfortunately titled *A Bird in the Bush*, and Mark Cocker's entertaining *Birders: Tales of a Tribe*. According to Moss, the history of birding is a story of obsession, male competition and male bonding, though the slim penultimate chapter, entitled 'Missing Out', at least acknowledges the absence of women, among other equally excluded groups. In *Tales of a Tribe*, published, like *A Bird in the Bush*, in the early 2000s, Cocker does not seem to notice the gap at all, although he does challenge the received notion that twentieth-century birdwatching was exclusively or even predominantly middle or upper class.

Cocker identifies fine and sometimes arcane distinctions among types of people interested in birds. Still, I'm not sure whether I can identify myself in any of the species and subspecies he so entertainingly describes. I'm not a 'twitcher', in the neutral, sometimes self-deprecating sense of the term used among birdwatchers themselves to describe a person who pursues rare sightings. I'm also certainly not a *birder* according to his classification system, and my exclusion from the birder category is because of feathers. 'Feathers,' he explains, 'are not just integral to a bird's identity, they are central to a birder's identity. No birder can be unaware of the existence or whereabouts of the submoustachial stripe or the tertials. You can be a birdwatcher, a bird-lover, a bird-spotter, a robin-stroker, even an ornithologist, but you're not a birder.' As it happens, I am aware of the existence and whereabouts of the submoustachial stripe and the tertials, but I could not spend any time talking about them. According to his taxonomy, though, birders can, and do. 'I know what they're saying,' he declares. 'They know what I'm talking about. Our identities are sheltered beneath the umbrella of those tertials. I belong. They belong.'

I don't belong in that way – and nor do I want to: not as a birder, not as a birdwatcher, or bird-spotter, or twitcher, or robin-stroker. But belonging isn't simply a matter of choice, of course. You can identify yourself as part of a particular group, but others both within and outside that group might not agree with how you see yourself. Similarly, others can identify you as belonging in a way that you reject. It seems self-evident that identity and belonging aren't binary qualities, yes or no, in or out – self-evident that they're socially determined, and vary according to context, and are often beyond your control – yet identity and belonging, inclusion and exclusion, can feel absolute.

I can't help rolling my eyes at the specialised coded language that birders or birdwatchers use without self-consciousness or irony, no matter where they fit in Cocker's system. But perhaps in some cases I'm judging a type of perception that I don't understand and don't know how to tolerate, reacting to expressions of neurodiversity that I conflate with the overbearing behaviour of many male birders: their competitiveness over rarities or numbers; their sounding off authoritatively; their explaining, without being asked, what you should be looking at and what you're seeing. I recoil from being talked over, from facial expressions of polite scepticism or disinterest, and above all from sentences that begin, implicitly or explicitly, with 'Actually, I think you'll find...'. In short, I recoil from birdsplaining, in all its easily identified plumage. Yet birdsplaining is precisely what I have done to the kind, friendly woman in the next bed.

The jackdaws settle on the roofs across the narrow road below me, and play among the terracotta chimney pots. There's no other word for what they're doing as they poke their heads into the openings to call *chack chack*, which must echo in interesting ways, though perhaps not so entertainingly for the buildings' inhabitants. I watch people pass. They never look up at the hospital windows, even when the windows are open, and the voice of a woman with dementia in a room off the main ward wails *help me, help me, help me, don't go, please don't go....*

The jackdaws preen one another endlessly, affectionately. I permit myself the projection of those human bonds in the absence of my own human bonds: here in hospital we have no contact, no visitors. Wales is heading into another wave of the pandemic, and there is covid at the gates, covid spreading on the wards.

The first night, I could not see out of the window. I was under close supervision by the bright lights of the nurses' station. My GP had sent me to A&E, and I'd been admitted to the cardiac ward after a CT scan confirmed a pulmonary embolism. I'd thought the swelling and pain in my leg was a torn calf muscle, which had happened before, but it had been a blood clot which subsequently travelled to my lungs. It was a strange word, *travelled*, I thought, in a quieter moment: as though the clot had bought a one-way ticket, packed a suitcase, and caught a train heading north. Which it had. Or rather *they* had: many of them had come to visit my lungs, and got stuck there, having nowhere else to go. I learned later, when I could bear to learn anything, that a pulmonary embolism is known as the sudden killer because it's often missed. Had my GP neglected to ask the critical question 'Any swelling or pain in your leg?' when I'd called to describe a severe shortness of breath and a worsening cough, the outcome might have been very different. For that question, and for his care afterwards, my GP has joined the ranks of my personal pantheon.

It was a Friday night, at about ten o'clock, when I was moved from A&E to the cardiac ward. All the patients lay with their backs to the windows, the beds facing in to the nurses' station. Behind me, on the north side of the hospital, the wide window would have shown me the empty car park, the occasional car or student heading up or down Penglais Hill, the dark huddle of the bluebell wood against the night sky, and herring gulls drifting silently past. It's one of the peculiarities of coastal towns at night, to be able to look up and see birds ghosting over, lit from below by the orange street lights. But I lay with my eyes closed against glaring white light, the blue curtains around my bed shutting out the sight but not the sound of the repeated emergencies going on around me. There was an unremitting noise of beeping monitors, which frequently shifted to loud summoning alarms. Then a nurse would come rushing, followed by an urgent cluster of doctors and doctor's assistants who carried out unspeakable interventions. The repeated medical emergency and distress of others on the ward, their privacy and mine stripped away, and the four-hourly visit from a nurse to check blood pressure and temperature and oxygen levels, made it impossible to concentrate, to read, to think, to sleep – to know anything at all except alarm and distress.

In the morning, I asked a nurse if my bed could be turned so that I could look out of the window. She gestured at the car park, and beyond it the rush-hour traffic heading downhill into town. 'Not much of a view,' she said. 'Yes, but it's outside,' I replied. The herring gulls, silenced by double or maybe triple glazing, had been joined by feral pigeons, and jackdaws, sometimes, and smaller birds too far off to identify, all getting on with the familiar, everyday business of survival.

She consulted, and came back to turn my bed as far as it could go – which was only a little way, maybe a 45-degree angle to the window, because of being hooked up to the heart monitor or the hazards of cables, or because otherwise it would disturb the order of the ward, so I sat on its edge and watched the gulls float by at eye level.

I wanted to look anywhere but at what was going on in the ward. The other three women were much worse off than I, so that I wondered what I was doing there, little realising then how serious my condition was. I was mobile. I could walk (slowly, carefully, breathlessly) to the toilet, but the other women were hooked up to drips, catheters, machines, and were too ill to move.

When my sister was twenty-one, she lay in hospital like that for three months, on her back with her leg in traction, after a bad car accident on the M25. She had not been wearing a seat belt, and was thrown across the carriageway into the path of oncoming traffic. She lay immobilised, with a bolt through her leg above the knee, while her splintered femur refused to knit. For three months, after overhearing a doctor's casual assessment, she lived in terror that her leg would be amputated. And although it wasn't – although in the end they successfully operated, pinning the bone in her leg, and another in her arm – she never recovered from the psychological injury it inflicted.

Given that experience of hospital trauma, that loss of autonomy, and the threat of medical decisions being made without her consent, it's no wonder that when she found a lump in her breast she put off going to a doctor until it was too late. I understood for the first time – trying to block out the intrusions and emergencies going on around me – why it had been impossible for her to engage in any way with the mechanised indignity and impersonality of the medical world; why it had been impossible for her to face what could happen – investigations and treatment that would violate the integrity of her body. No wonder that she opted instead for a determined belief in her body's capacity to 'naturally' heal itself from cancer, and sought out so-called 'natural' remedies (among them natural poisons) to help her body in its work. Perhaps, after all, her rejection of medical intervention wasn't only about fear; perhaps it gave her a sense of personal control and resilience in the face of fear.

That first night and day in hospital, with a cannula in my arm, 'in case', listening to what was happening around me, I was terrified of what 'they' were going to do to me, too. But it was not an anonymous white-coated 'them': the doctor on call was the doctor who had seen me in A&E, and he was kind, patient, had taken his time, had broken the serious news to me gently, by degrees. And while I was filled with dread by the invasive investigations and treatments that he and others casually named as possibilities, I was as terrified of what my body was doing all by itself, naturally.

After that night and morning under close watch,

my bed was wheeled down the corridor to a much quieter ward with the view of the jackdaws. The ward sister came bustling in after me. 'Would you like the spot by the window?' she asked. 'I noticed that you wanted to see out.' She too joined my growing personal pantheon, alongside my GP, and the respiratory doctor who'd admitted me. And so I lay and watched the jackdaws that evening until the lights in the ward reflecting off the dark windows made it difficult to see outside. After they were dimmed at ten o'clock, I lay on my side and looked out at the night sky, at stars.

The Dyfi ward, where I had fetched up, is named after a river, as are several others in the hospital – the Leri, the Ystwyth, the Rheidol. That invocation of running water seemed appropriate, as I lay awake hoping for my blood to flow normally again, and my heart and my lungs to go back to doing their work without scrutiny, without assistance, naturally.

The sense of the natural, when it comes to my body, is intimately tied to a deliberate ignorance of its internal workings (except, of course, the ones I must consciously attend to: sex and reproduction; the intake of fuel; the expulsion of waste, and the repair of surface damage). The body uninvestigated is a pristine *terra incognita*. I have at most an overview of its geographical features from the vantage point of its border, the skin. In order for it to remain in its 'natural' state, which is to say seemingly working in harmony and balance, its interior, under the skin, must stay unexplored: a protected area of wilderness, a conservation area. To subject the interior to scrutiny, to the opening up of scientific knowledge, is to risk contaminating it, and changing it.

The natural versus the artificial; the normal versus the aberrant; balance and harmony versus invasion and change: all the old established binaries that are routinely, unthinkingly applied to the so-called natural world seem also to apply to our bodies – or at least they seem to apply to mine.

The idea of the natural and harmonious, as against the invasive and destructive, must colour most people's physical sense of themselves, wherever their personal norm lies along a distribution of health and illness, of ability and disability (it feels impossible to describe the distribution of physical and medical variation without the pejorative associations that even the most objective statistical vocabulary carries: *norm*, *normal*, *abnormal*, *deviation*, and, by extension, *ability*, *disability*).

Of course unlike me, some people are curious about their own bodies rather than squeamish;

some rely on scrutiny and intervention to survive, to function, to thrive, and some rely on it from birth onwards. For others, the urgency about protecting the body's integrity and autonomy is powerfully felt – particularly, as was the case with my sister, if they have experienced medical trauma, or their social or psychological or sexual integrity and autonomy has been violated or is under threat.

Anyone confronted by their body declaring itself in alarming and unfamiliar ways must long for the restoration of its apparently natural – which is to say familiar – state: the sense that it is working normally, and therefore its invisible internal parts and processes can be ignored. What I felt about the medical intervention I was facing as I lay in my hospital bed wasn't only fear of physical discomfort or pain. My need to restore a sense of my body's natural state, a state of purported normality, was in some way a desire to return to ignorance, or innocence: I wanted once again to be unaware of its interior, and of its hidden labour.

Perhaps a sense of the body as your own personal Eden under threat provides one of the emotional charges behind the fear of vaccines during the Covid-19 pandemic, as is the case with parents who see their children as existing in some kind of primal, natural state which any vaccine might violate. At the start of the Covid-19 vaccination programme, and throughout the first two years of the pandemic, the imagery of the body, in all the pop-science permutations and media shortcuts, was one of war zone rather than wilderness. T-cells and antibodies and all the variants of immune response were depicted in the language of defence and surveillance, of infiltrating or bypassing security systems, and of search-and-destroy missions, while vaccines themselves were repeatedly characterised as weapons, part of an 'arsenal' in a war.

Maybe the repeated imagery of the body as a battlefield, in a continual state of invasion and counter-attack, of contamination and clean-up, helped to reinforce for some the need to defend the body against all imperial and military intervention, and reinforced the notion of the body as the very last bit of 'unspoiled' nature that we have left. But what a painful (and often fatal) irony it has been to embrace an idea of the immune system as natural, harmonious, and above all trustworthy in the face of what seems out of control and disempowering, when that 'natural' system, inflamed into hyperactivity by Covid-19 infection, can itself become such a very dangerous liability.

That idea of a personal Eden might provide

comfort and guidance when you're confronted by what seems like authoritarian medical threat, but of course no one's body is a pristine, original wilderness. The body is shaped by human knowledge and human experience, even if much of the time its interior, or hinterland, is a wilderness, in the sense that it goes largely unnoted and unmonitored.

It's to that state of unobserved wilderness that I longed to return, as I lay on my side and watched the jackdaws, and the following morning, and every morning, saw a kite drifting down from the National Library towards the hospital and out of sight above me. Unmarked by the kind of trauma my sister had undergone, I was lucky to be able to trust that medical treatment – developed by the authoritarian might of so-called Big Pharma – could help rather than disrupt my body's natural processes, and could give my body the support it needed while it got on with the task of clearing blockages, opening pathways, and beginning the work of returning to its normal state.

When I came home from hospital I could not walk ten metres without resting, weak and light-headed and out of breath. Before the onset of symptoms that I now recognise were early signs of things going wrong, I was running ten kilometres with little effort. 'Telegraph pole by telegraph pole,' the cardiac consultant had told me. 'You must take it slowly.' So I did. And I spent my time birdwatching, during that recovery, in a way I'd never watched birds before: from inside, at the window; standing at field gates; leaning against fence posts or trees; sitting on whatever nearest wet rock or sodden bench presented itself when I suddenly needed it, or walking slowly, so slowly, step by step, a little further every day.

And I watched a bird inside the house, too – because, at the end of the first pandemic lockdown, finally, at the age of fifty-two, I had bought a parrot.

Though I've bird-proofed each room as best I can, having a parrot is like having a winged two-year-old in the house. If there's something she can damage or be damaged by, she'll find it. Mostly I spend time taking things away from her: my coffee, pens (now that she's worked out how to remove – and swallow – the ballpoint), my glasses, my binoculars (but not before she'd scalloped the soft rubber parts). She can make short work of unclipping keyboard keys, or removing phonepad buttons. Though I provide her with natural toys made of wood, of materials she can shred, she's more interested in tech, particularly black tech: mobile phones, wiring, plugs, small metal objects, which she explores thoroughly with her dexterous, destructive beak.

She is about four and a half inches long, and blue – her underparts cerulean, her rump and back and tail feathers turquoise, her tertials slate-coloured with a turquoise sheen. At first her tail was stubby – she had only recently fledged when I'd brought her home – but when her tail feathers grew in they were pointed and stiff, like a woodpecker's, or those of a treecreeper.

Blue isn't a very common colour in birds, which is perhaps why it seems so remarkable when I see it. In the UK, it's only ever part of a bird's variegated colouring: a teal or a jay's patch of feathers; a kingfisher's flash of turquoise and rust; a swallow's deep blue-black back and wings, if seen at the right angle; a magpie's blue-green sheen in certain lights. Even the blue tit is largely yellow. California is a bit more generous with blue, both in its kingfishers and its jays: the belted kingfisher's head and breastband a slatey blue; stellar's jays blue all over, shading to black on their crested heads; scrub jays with their blue elements. The saturated colour of the western bluebird, the first time I saw one, in the Sunol Wilderness, seemed unnatural, as if it had been dipped in dye.

The cerulean and turquoise of this four-and-a-half-inch parrotlet *is* unnatural, in a sense: female celestial or Pacific parrotlets are green in the wild, but in captivity they've been selectively bred for colour for at least a century.

It was not until after I came home from hospital that I realised her colouring was similar to the budgie my sister had owned when she was young. It seemed that, even years after her death, I was still following her choices, as I had done, annoyingly, when we were children. There was the occasion (for which she never forgave me) when I trailed with my mother into every clothes shop in Brighton in search of a new coat, and in the end came back to the first choice: the same baseball jacket that my sister had chosen, though I had to opt for a different colour. Unimaginatively, I also mimicked her imaginary country, Greenland (inhabited by galloping silver brumbies), with my own version, Redland (also inhabited by wild brumbies), although she pointed out that Redland was actually a brick factory (Redland lorries, transporting bricks from the works at Crowhurst or Godstone, were a regular sight when we were young).

At first, as I rested and recovered from illness, I observed my blue parrotlet as I had never done before, noting the gradation of colour across her wing feathers, the variation within each feather, comparing her careful labour of preening with the preening I'd watched the jackdaws engage in, and delighting in her irrepressible curiosity as she insisted on investigating with her beak everything my hands did – or every object she was forbidden. She had a particular enthusiastic chirrup if she spotted my binoculars; I would know from two rooms away if I had accidently left them lying in sight.

Every day, I walked further, slowly: first round the garden, then twice a day, morning and night. Then to the postbox, and afterwards to the second street light; later to the church, and then as far as the horses' paddock, the council houses, and finally up the hill to Spite Cottage, a holiday home just beyond the fork in the road. The 'Spite' of the building's name is to do with respite rather than spitefulness, and its etymology – from ysbyty, meaning hostel, hospitality and, in modern Welsh, hospital – resonated strongly for me as the cottage marked a point of respite at the top of the steep slope out of the village. Perhaps it was once a resting place on the way to the Cistercian abbey of Ystrad Fflur, or for drovers heading for Tregaron, and, eventually, London. When I reached it that first time, I thought – ambitiously, determined, hopeful – that one day sometime in the next twelve months I would run the eight miles to Tregaron, working up to it, telegraph pole by telegraph pole, gate by gate, mile by mile.

For weeks, I walked everywhere with binoculars, slowly, carefully, resting along the way, first accompanied by my partner, then by my younger daughter, who'd travelled from Berlin to look after me, and then alone, eventually making it up the steep hill to the common, which marked my first mile. There – the reward for pushing myself to go just a little bit further, despite the wind – I saw a peregrine at close quarters, putting all the fieldfares to nervous flight. It was unmistakeably a peregrine, which, for a luxurious long moment, leaning against a cold metal gate, I watched skimming over low above me. There was no mistaking that thick black moustachial stripe.

I might not be ready to spend hours discussing moustachial stripes or tertials or fine points of identification, and I might not ever keep a list of birds I've seen, but something has changed: I'm ready to claim it, at last, my identity as a birdwatcher. Somehow, now, I don't mind belonging – I might even want to belong, if they'll have me.

Perhaps my change of attitude is because of the birds that saw me through while I was in hospital, and afterwards, during my recovery. Perhaps it is because the experience of being in hospital, where all your dignity and privacy are stripped away, has taught me how unimportant embarrassment is, in the end. But mostly it is down to being treated with kindness – by people who didn't know me, and by people who did, including birdwatchers: both kindness at the time, and for months afterwards.

The kindness of others has made me reflect on my own habits of unkindness in thought, in attitude, and on my tendency to judge. 'Everything good in the world is kindness,' Jan Morris said, in her last interview before she died. 'If you are not sure what you think about something, the most useful questions are these.... Are you being kind? Are they being kind? That usually gives you the answer.' It seems good advice for life generally, though curiously I remember it as an instruction: 'Be kind.'

Notes and Bibliographical Details

Birdsplaining: A Note Before Reading
For the origins of mansplaining, see salon. com/2014/05/20/men_explain_things_to_me_the_ author_behind_mansplaining_on_the_origin_of_ her_famous_coinage/.

For an account and image of the statue, see dailydot.com/irl/san-antonio-statue-illustrates-mansplaining/.

1. Reading the Signs
There is a great deal of literature on birds in folklore, but relatively little that combines an expertise in both birds and folkloristics. Venetia Newall's *Discovering the Folklore of Birds and Beasts* (Shire, 1971) offers just that.

2. Field Guides
The older field guides described here are Hermann Heinzel, Richard Fitter and John Parslow, *The Birds of*

Britain and Europe with North Africa and the Middle East (Collins, 1972) and Roger Peterson, Guy Mountfort and PAD Hollom, *A Field Guide to the Birds of Britain and Europe* (Collins, 1954). The five hardback volumes of 'Witherby's' [HF Witherby, FCR Jourdain, Norman F Ticehurst and Bernard W Tucker, *The Handbook of British Birds* (Witherby, 1941)] are too numerous and heavy to take anywhere, but they are a beautiful and invaluable identification resource – particularly when annotated, as mine is, with tiny fountain-pen corrections and additions by an anonymous Scottish birdwatcher. Barbara and Richard Mearns' *Biographies for Birdwatchers: The Lives of Those Commemorated in Western Palearctic Bird Names* (Academic Press, 1988) is an equally heavy and informative (if dated) resource on identifying the individuals behind bird names, while more recent and less gendered field guides include Peter Holden and Tim Cleeves, *RSPB Handbook of British Birds* (Bloomsbury, 2002; 2014), and Paul Sterry and Paul Stancliffe, *Collins BTO Guide to British Birds* (Collins, 2015).

3. Mansplaining the Wild

Jim Hinch's article 'Nature Writing is Over' was originally published in the *LA Review of Books* in 2012 and republished in *Salon* (28 July, 2013). It can be accessed online at salon.com. Mark Cocker's *Crow Country: A Meditation on Birds, Landscape and Nature* was published by Vintage in 2008. Kathleen Jamie's much-quoted article, 'A Lone Enraptured Male', appeared in the *London Review of Books* on 6 March, 2008. Other works mentioned are Helen Macdonald, *H is for Hawk* (Jonathan Cape, 2014); Robert Macfarlane, *The Wild Places* (Penguin, 2007), and Cheryl Strayed, *Wild: From Lost to Found on the Pacific Crest Trail* (Knopf, 2012).

4. Boggy Ground

Cors Caron is managed by Natural Resources Wales – see naturalresources.wales. TH White's *The Once and Future King* was published by Collins in 1958, and has appeared in multiple editions since then. His earlier book, *The Goshawk*, was published by Jonathan Cape, in 1951, and, following the success of *H is for Hawk*, was republished in 2015 by Weidenfeld & Nicolson in a beautiful hardback edition with an introduction by Helen Macdonald. The film *The Fisher King*, directed by Terry Gilliam (TriStar Pictures), was released in 1991. The original documents and history of Rothschild's Society for the Promotion of Nature Reserves are published on the Wildlife Trusts' website: wildlifetrusts.org/about-us/rothschilds-list.

5. Curious Bodies
Kathleen Jamie's *Findings* was published by Sort of Books in 2005, and Mary Oliver's poems, 'I Found a Dead Fox' and 'Wings', appear in her volume *White Pine* (Harcourt Brace & Company, 1994). Jaime De Angulo's *Indian Tales* was published by AA Wyn in 1953. Other books mentioned here are Niall Griffiths, *Sheepshagger* (Jonathan Cape, 2001); Thom Gunn, *Boss Cupid* (Farrar Strauss Giroux, 2000) and *The Man with Night Sweats* (Farrar Strauss Giroux, 1992); Joy Harjo's *A Map to the Next World: Poetry and Tales* (Norton, 2000), and *How We Became Human: New and Selected Poems, 1975–2001* (Norton, 2002).

6. Uninvited Guests
The Mammal Society's scat guide is available on their website at mammal.org.uk/whose-poo/ and the RSPB's guide, 'Give Nature a Home', can be accessed at rspb.org.uk/Images/GNaH%20Guide_tcm9-348105.pdf. Hugh Warwick (@hedgehoghugh) reported in a tweet in 2019: 'Once, when asked in a TV interview how to help hedgehogs, I answered with "we need to dismantle industrial capitalism" – interviewer's face went pale – and then recovered as she remembered it was a pre-record and it never troubled the viewers

with being broadcast' (twitter.com/hedgehoghugh/
status/1100687765019283456).

7. Meetings at Dusk

Chris Cooper's experience was widely covered in
the press. The CBS News piece, '"That act was
unmistakably racist": Christian Cooper speaks out
after viral encounter with white dog-walker', includes
a video interview on 10 June, 2020, cbsnews.com/
news/amy-cooper-christian-cooper-speaks-out-that-
act-was-unmistakably-racist/.

The latest information about Black Birders Week,
hosted by the Black AF in STEM collective, can be
found at blackafinstem.com.

For details of the national competition to choose
the UK's favourite nature writing book, see 'Land
Lines: Finding the UK's Favourite Book about Nature'
(undated) ahrc.ukri.org/favouritenaturebooks.

Richard Smyth's 'The Dark Side of Nature Writing'
appeared in *New Humanist* on 20 June, 2018, and an
expanded and updated version, 'Nature Writing's
Fascist Roots', was published in the *New Statesman* on
3 April, 2019 (newstatesman.com/culture/2019/04/
nature-writings-fascist-roots).

Details about Henry Williamson, author of
Tarka the Otter: His Joyful Water-Life and Death in

the Country of the Two Rivers (GP Putnam's Sons, 1927), can be found on the Henry Williamson society website, henrywilliamson.co.uk.

There are many unsourced online references to nightjar beliefs, but one of the more reliable is Logan Parker, 'Milk Thieves and Harbingers of Doom?' – a Short History of Nightjar Folklore', published by the Maine Nightjar Monitoring Project, 9 December, 2019 (mainenightjar.com/post/nightjar-folklore). The vampire association is reinforced by the tradition that Venetia Newall records in *Discovering the Folklore of Birds and Beasts* (Shire, 1971): 'In Somerset it was a witch in disguise, which drains the cattle dry and can only be destroyed by a gun loaded with a silver sixpence.' See also the nightjar entry in E and MA Radford, *The Encyclopedia of Superstitions*, edited by Christine Hole (Hutchinson, 1980), and for the uncanny (with no reference to nightjars), see Freud's essay in translation at mit.edu/allanmc/www/freud1.pdf.

8. What's in a Name?

The birdheistboys' photo can be seen on Twitter (twitter. com/N8Swick/status/1283412575103979520), and the hashtag #BlackBirdersWeek will bring up many examples on Twitter and Instagram.

For information about Bird Names for Birds, see birdnamesforbirds.wordpress.com.

For information about Tristram's ornithology, see WG Hale's exclusively ornithological biography, *Sacred Ibis: The Ornithology of Canon Henry Baker Tristram, DD, FRS* (Sacristy Press, 2016), which, among other details, traces the path of Tristram's collections. Jonathan Rosen's *The Life of the Skies: Birding at the End of Nature* (Picador, 2008) also has two chapters on Tristram, and there is a brief discussion of him in Paul Armstrong, *The English Parson-Naturalist: A Companionship between Science and Religion* (Gracewing, 2000). Philip Sclater's formal naming of the Tristram's grackle appeared in *The Annals and Magazine of Natural History*, Volume 2, Series 3 (1858), pp 465–466.

Tristram's works are out of print, but several – including *The Land of Israel: A Journal of Travels in Palestine, Undertaken with Special Reference to Its Physical Character* (1865) – went into multiple editions. *The Natural History of the Bible* was published in 1867, and *The Land of Moab: Travels and Discoveries on the East Side of the Dead Sea and the Jordan* in 1873. Some of his books are available in print-on-demand form (otherwise they are rather expensive: a copy of his *Fauna and Flora of Western Palestine* was on sale in 2022 for £1500). His articles in *Ibis*, including his rather defensive later communications, are available to read through a Wiley subscription.

For information on the Debatable Lands (and the origin of blackmail), see Graham Robb, *The Debatable Land: The Lost World Between Scotland and England* (Picador, 2018).

The author of the *Daily Mail* article, 'Now Wokism is Coming for the Birds!', was Hailey Richardson. See dailymail.co.uk/femail/article-9792411/Campaigners-call-bird-names-links-colonialism-changed.html (15 July, 2021).

For *Biographies for Birdwatchers*, see Chapter 2, Field Guides.

9. The Promise of Puffins
Skomer Island is run by the Wildlife Trust of South and West Wales – see welshwildlife.org/ – and the Mull Eagle Watch project is run by a partnership comprised of the Mull and Iona Community Trust, RSPB Scotland, Scottish Natural Heritage, and Police Scotland – see mulleaglewatch.com/.

10. To Gawp at Birds
For the Dyfi Osprey Project, including livestreaming during the breeding season, see dyfiospreyproject.

com/. Other works cited here are Richard Mabey's introduction to Gilbert White, *The Natural History of Selborne* (1789; Penguin, 1977); Mark Cocker's 'Death of the Naturalist: Why is the "New Nature Writing" So Tame?', published in the *New Statesman*, 17 June, 2015 (online at newstatesman.com), and Charlotte Chambers, '"Well It's Remote, I Suppose, Innit?" The relational politics of birdwatching through the CCTV lens', in *Scottish Geographical Journal* 123.2 (June 2007), pp 122–134. Charles Foster's *The Screaming Sky* (Little Toller) appeared in 2021, and Mark Cocker's *Birders: Tales of a Tribe* (Vintage) in 2002.

12. Gannets

Access information and firing times for Castlemartin can be found on the UK Government website, gov.uk/government/publications/castlemartin-firing-notice—2. The BMC's description has been removed from the website, but appears in slightly amended form on the bouldering forum, ukbouldering.com (ukbouldering.com/board/index.php?topic=31183.0).

13. Risk Assessment

For the NHS definition of agoraphobia, see nhs.uk/mental-health/conditions/agoraphobia/overview/.

14. An Unkindness to Birdwatchers

The Winterwatch barn owl footage can be seen on Springwatch's Twitter feed for 27 January, 2021 (twitter. com/bbcspringwatch/status/1354522126729019395).

The *xkcd* comic strip, 'Duty Calls', is published online at xkcd.com/386/. The *Midsomer Murders* episode featuring the blue-crested hoopoe was broadcast on 11 January, 2012. Both birdforum.net and community. rspb.org.uk feature discussion threads about its outrages.

The research on boredom, 'Boring People: Stereotype Characteristics, Interpersonal Attributions, and Social Reactions', by Wijnand AP van Tilburg, Eric R Igou and Mehr Panjwani, was published on 8 March, 2022 (see journals.sagepub.com/doi/full/10. 1177/01461672221079104). The reports appeared on 15 March, 2022, in *The Week* (theweek.co.uk/news/world-news/956085/worlds-most-boring-people-revealed), and on 19 March, 2022, in *The Observer* (Viv Groskop, 'If You Find Everyone Else Boring You Only Have Yourself to Blame', theguardian.com). Mark Cocker's classification system can be found on pages 24 and 25 in *Birders: Tales of a Tribe*; Stephen Moss' *A Bird in the Bush: A Social History of Birdwatching* was published by Aurum Press in 2004, and Tim Adams' interview with Jan Morris was published in *The Observer* on St David's Day, 2020.

Acknowledgements

An excerpt, 'Reading the Signs', appeared in issue 127 of *New Welsh Reader* in autumn 2021. Early versions of some passages in this book were originally drafted during the period of a Creative Wales Award in 2015 – thanks to the Arts Council of Wales for that support. My thanks also to Dave Sexton, Hugh Dignon, Don, Sarah, and Ally for their help in Scotland, and to Kirsti and Ian in Wales.

Mike Parker provided the best kind of critical and writerly response to a late draft of the text, for which I am hugely grateful. Thanks also to Gwen Davies for her sustained and patient engagement, careful shaping, and always thoughtful challenge.

My daughters, with whom I have explored most of the ideas in this book, have offered me invaluable encouragement and insight, as well as close reading. My thanks to Simka for crucial feedback on an early essay, and to Jericha for sagacious feedback on the whole.

Finally, my thanks to Tony, for belaying me through good and ill.